Contents

Thanks

We would like to thank all those dedicated Italian teachers who have worked closely and constructively with us on these materials over many years. Special thanks are due to Jeremy Hunter for seeing the typescript through its several versions.

JM
RB

X

Reading between the lines

Reading between the lines

Integrated language and
literature activities

*John McRae and
Roy Boardman*

 CAMBRIDGE
UNIVERSITY PRESS

PUBLISHED BY THE PRESS SYNDICATE OF THE UNIVERSITY OF CAMBRIDGE
The Pitt Building, Trumpington Street, Cambridge CB2 1RP, United Kingdom

CAMBRIDGE UNIVERSITY PRESS
The Edinburgh Building, Cambridge CB2 2RU, United Kingdom
40 West 20th Street, New York, NY 10011–4211, USA
10 Stamford Road, Oakleigh, Melbourne 3166, Australia

First published 1984
Fourteenth printing 1998

Printed in the United Kingdom at the University Press, Cambridge

Library of Congress catalogue card number: 84–4262

British Library cataloguing in publication data

McRae, John

Reading between the lines.
1. English language – Text-books for foreign
speakers
I. Title   II. Boardman, Roy
428.2'4   P1128

ISBN 0 521 27789 2 Student's Book
ISBN 0 521 27790 6 Teacher's Book
ISBN 0 521 25992 4 Set of 2 cassettes

To the student

This book does exactly what its title and sub-title suggest: it helps you to see below the surface (between the lines) of what you read in English, and to improve your own ability in the language (in particular, your fluency) by offering many wide-ranging opportunities to practise. To this end, it introduces you to English literature, to what writers have told us about their experience of life, their feelings and opinions, in ages as far apart as William Shakespeare's and Samuel Beckett's. You will find that the literary texts deepen and enrich your thinking and feeling and result in more effective personal expression.

At the same time, you will begin to read English poetry and prose with pleasure and understanding. The book does all it can to bring literature not only within your grasp, but also into direct relation with the things you most care about.

Books are good enough in their own way, but they are a mighty bloodless substitute for life.

Robert Louis Stevenson, *Virginibus Puerisque*

1 Family

We're a family, aren't we?

1.1 Theme 📼

Listen to the song and decide who you more easily identify with, the father or the son.

Father

It's not time to make a change
Just relax, take it easy
You're still young, that's your fault
There's so much you have to know
Find a girl, settle down
If you want you can marry
Look at me, I am old
But I'm happy

I was once like you are now
And I know that it's not easy
To be calm when you've found
Something going on
But take your time, think a lot
Why think of everything you've got
For you will still be here tomorrow
But your dreams may not

Son

How can I try to explain
When I do he turns away again
It's always been the same
Same old story
From the moment I could talk
I was ordered to listen
Now there's a way and I know
That I have to go away
I know I have to go

1

Family

It's not time to make a change
Just sit down and take it slowly
You're still young, that's your fault
There's so much you have to go
    through
Find a girl, settle down
If you want you can marry
Look at me, I am old
But I'm happy

Stay, stay,
        stay
Why must
        you go and make this
            decision
Alone?

Away, away,
            away
I know

            I have to make this decision
Alone –

        no

All the times that I've cried
Keeping all the things I knew inside
It's hard, but it's harder
To ignore it
If they were right I'd agree
But it's them they know not me
Now there's a way and I know
That I have to go away
I know I have to go

Cat Stevens, 'Father and Son'

Discuss these points with a partner.
a) The father's attitude to his son, and the son's attitude to his father. Which do you more easily identify with?
b) Have you ever experienced this kind of relationship with a parent or a child?
c) Is the son right to leave home? What circumstances would justify doing so? Are there any circumstances which would make leaving home impossible to justify?

1.2 Discuss your thoughts, conclusions and experiences with the class as a whole. Can you think of other problems that families often have? Do they differ at all from country to country? Or from one part of your country to another? Make a list and a few notes on how common you think each problem is.

2.1 Text A 📼

As you read, look for the answers to the following questions:
a) Why is the father an outsider in the home?
b) How old is Paul?
c) What does Paul dislike most about his father?
d) Can we ever see a positive side to the father's nature?

'Wha's it matter to yo' what time I come whoam?' he shouted.

And everybody in the house was still, because he was danger-ous. He ate his food in the most brutal manner possible and, when he had done, pushed all the pots in a heap away from him, to lay his arms on the table. Then he went to sleep. 5

Paul hated his father so. The collier's small, mean head, with its black hair slightly soiled with grey, lay on the bare arms, and the face, dirty and inflamed, with a fleshy nose and thin, paltry brows, was turned sideways, asleep with beer and weariness 10 and nasty temper. If anyone entered suddenly, or a noise were made, the man looked up and shouted:

'I'll lay my fist about thy y'ead, I'm tellin' thee, if tha doesna stop that clatter! Dost hear?'

And the two last words, shouted in a bullying fashion, 15 usually at Annie, made the family writhe with hate of the man.

He was shut out from all family affairs. No one told him any-thing. The children, alone with their mother, told her all about the day's happenings, everything. Nothing had really taken place in them until it was told to their mother. But as soon as the 20 father came in, everything stopped. He was like the scotch in the smooth, happy machinery of the home. And he was always aware of this fall of silence on his entry, the shutting off of life, the unwelcome. But now it was gone too far to alter.

He would dearly have liked the children to talk to him, but 25 they could not. Sometimes Mrs Morel would say:

'You ought to tell your father.'

Paul won a prize in a competition in a child's paper. Every-body was highly jubilant.

'Now you'd better tell your father when he comes in,' said 30 Mrs Morel. 'You know how he carries on and says he's never told anything.'

'All right,' said Paul. But he would almost rather have for-feited the prize than have to tell his father.

'I've won a prize in a competition, dad,' he said. 35

Morel turned round to him.

⇛→

3

'Have you, my boy? What sort of a competition?'
'Oh, nothing – about famous women.'
'And how much is the prize, then, as you've got?'
'It's a book.'   40
'Oh, indeed!'
'About birds.'
'Hm – hm!'
And that was all. Conversation was impossible between the
father and any other member of the family. He was an outsider.   45
He had denied the God in him.

The only times when he entered again into the life of his own
people was when he worked, and was happy at work. Sometimes, in the evening, he cobbled the boots or mended the kettle
or his pit-bottle. Then he always wanted several attendants,   50
and the children enjoyed it. They united with him in the work,
in the actual doing of something, when he was his real self
again.

He was a good workman, dexterous, and one who, when he
was in a good humour, always sang. He had whole periods,   55
months, almost years, of friction and nasty temper. Then sometimes he was jolly again. It was nice to see him run with a piece
of red-hot iron into the scullery, crying:

'Out of my road – out of my road!'

Then he hammered the soft, red-glowing stuff on his iron   60
goose, and made the shape he wanted. Or he sat absorbed for a
moment, soldering. Then the children watched with joy as the
metal sank suddenly molten, and was shoved about against the
nose of the soldering-iron, while the room was full of a scent of
burnt resin and hot tin, and Morel was silent and intent for a   65
minute. He always sang when he mended boots because of the
jolly sound of hammering. And he was rather happy when he
sat putting great patches on his moleskin pit trousers, which he
would often do, considering them too dirty, and the stuff too
hard, for his wife to mend.   70

D.H. Lawrence, *Sons and Lovers*

Discuss the answers you have found to the questions, before going on,
and, if you wish, relate each one to your personal experience of family
life by talking about the following points with a partner. The letters (a)
to (d) relate the points to the questions you have answered.
a) Think of an outsider in your own family, or in a family you know
   well. What is his/her influence on family life?

b) Is it common at Paul's age for young people to feel they hate their fathers and mothers, or conversely have a very strong attachment to them?

c) Have *you* ever felt strong dislike for a parent's behaviour or attitudes? What attitudes does the son dislike in Cat Stevens's song?

d) What are the positive sides of *your own* nature, do you think, from the point of view of other members of your family?

2.2 Discuss the following in groups of three or four and make notes on your conclusions. Then compare ideas.

a) The father is presented very unfavourably. Do we have any sympathy for him? When, and how is it brought out?

b) The first reference in the passage to Mr Morel is to 'his father'. What other words are used to refer to him? Why does Lawrence keep changing?

c) Why do you think the father acts as he does? Do you feel he realises what the others think of him?

d) What do you imagine the relationship between Paul's mother and father is like?

e) Do you find the passage realistic, or exaggerated?

f) There are several possible 'gaps' in communication in this family scene, any of which might help to explain how the situation arose. Which of the following do you think the most significant in the context?
  – the generation gap
  – inability to communicate because of different social backgrounds and working environments
  – unwillingness to communicate
  – shyness
  – insecurity
  Discuss the relevance of each of these possibilities and any others you think are important.

2.3 Look carefully at the way Lawrence constructs his paragraphs in relation to each other, and discuss their effectiveness in relation to the theme. In particular, notice that:
  – Three paragraphs begin with 'And', one with 'Then'.
  – Several paragraphs begin with the names of the characters or with a personal pronoun.
  – All the paragraphs in the conversation between Paul and his father (Morel) are one-line, single-sentence paragraphs.
  – The final paragraph of the extract is longer than all the others.

2.4 Basically, the past tense used in the extract has two meanings. One meaning is that of 'used to do', the other refers to events that occurred only once.
a) Find out where these different meanings occur and comment on the contrast between them.
b) What is the effect of the phrase: 'Sometimes Mrs Morel *would say...*'?

2.5 a) The vocabulary that Lawrence chooses is strong, simple, direct. Find those words that you think are most effective, and try to say why you find them so.
b) Compare Lawrence's style in describing Mr Morel to Charles Dickens's style in describing Mr Gradgrind.

Mr Morel

The collier's small, mean head, with its black hair slightly soiled with grey, lay on the bare arms, and the face, dirty and inflamed, with a fleshy nose and thin, paltry brows, was turned sideways, asleep with beer and weariness and nasty temper.

Mr Gradgrind

The emphasis was helped by the speaker's square wall of a forehead, which had his eyebrows for its base, while his eyes found commodious cellarage in two dark caves, overshadowed by the wall. The emphasis was helped by the speaker's mouth, which was wide, thin, and hard set. The emphasis was helped by the speaker's voice, which was inflexible, dry, and dictatorial. The emphasis was helped by the speaker's hair, which bristled on the skirts of his bald head, a plantation of firs to keep the wind from its shining surface, all covered with knobs, like the crust of a plum pie, as if the head had scarcely warehouse-room for the hard facts stored inside.

Charles Dickens, *Hard Times*

One of the differences is the absence of simile and metaphor in Lawrence's description, and their frequent occurrence in the Dickens piece. Can you suggest reasons why the authors might have made such different choices?

3.1 Text B 🔲

As you read and listen to this scene, try to work out the relationship between the characters.

HARRY [*he is hurt and throws a hand at her in disgust*]: Ach! you make me sick.

SARAH [*mocking*]: Ach, you make me sick. *I* make *him* sick. Him, my fine man! You're the reason why she thinks like this, you know that?

HARRY: Yes, me.

SARAH: Well, of course you. Who else?

RONNIE [*collecting dishes and escaping to the kitchen*]: I'll wash up.

HARRY: I didn't bring her up – she's all your work.

SARAH: That's just it! You didn't bring her up. You weren't concerned, were you? You left it all to me while you went to your mother's or to the pictures or out with your friends.

HARRY: Yes. I went out with my friends. Sure!

SARAH: Well, didn't you? May I have so many pennies for the times you went up West to pictures.

HARRY: Oh, leave off, Sarah.

SARAH: Leave off! That's all he can say – leave off, leave me alone. That was it. I did leave you alone. That's why I had all the trouble.

ADA: I'm going home, Mummy.

SARAH [*caressingly and apologetically*]: Oh no, Ada, stay, it's early yet. Stay. We'll play solo.

ADA: I'm feeling tired and I must write to Dave.

SARAH: Well, stay here and write to Dave. We'll all be quiet. Ronnie's going out. Daddy'll go to bed and I've got some washing to do. Stay, Ada, stay. What do you want to rush home for? A cold, miserable, two-roomed flat, all on your own. Stay. We're a family aren't we?

ADA [*putting on her coat*]: I've also got washing to do, I must go –

SARAH: I'll do it for you. What's a mother for? Straight from work I'll go to your place and bring it back with me. Stay. You've got company here – perhaps Uncle Hymie and Auntie Lottie'll come up. What do you want to be on your own for, tell me?

ADA: I'm not *afraid* of being on my own – I must go.

SARAH [*wearily*]: Go then! Will we see you tomorrow?

ADA: Yes, I'll come for supper tomorrow night. Good night. [*Calling*] Good night, Ronnie.

RONNIE [*appearing from kitchen*]: 'Night, Addy.

SARAH: You washing up, Ronnie?

RONNIE: I'm washing up.

SARAH: You I don't have to worry about – but your sister runs ⋙→

away. At the first sight of a little bother she runs away. Why does she run away, Ronnie? Before she used to sit and discuss things, now she runs to her home – such a home to run to – two rooms and a shadow!

RONNIE: But, Ma, she's a married woman herself. You think she hasn't her own worries wondering what it'll be like to see Dave after all these years?

SARAH: But you never run away from a discussion. At least I've got you around to help me solve problems.

RONNIE: Mother, my one virtue – if I got any at all – is that I always imagine you can solve things by talking about them – ask my form master! [*Returns to kitchen.*]

SARAH [*wearily to Harry*]: You see what you do? That's your daughter. Not a word from her father to ask her to stay. The family doesn't matter to you. All your life you've let the family fall around you, but it doesn't matter to you.

HARRY: I didn't drive her away.

SARAH [*bitterly*]: No – you didn't drive her away. How could you? You were the good, considerate father.

    [HARRY *turns away and hunches himself up miserably.*]

Look at you! Did you shave this morning? Look at the cigarette ash on the floor. Your shirt! When did you last change your shirt? He sits. Nothing moves him, nothing worries him. He sits! A father! A husband!

HARRY [*taking out a cigarette to light*]: Leave me alone, please leave me alone, Sarah. You started the row, not me, you!

SARAH [*taking cigarette from his hand*]: Why must you always smoke? – talk with me. Talk, talk, Harry.

HARRY: Sarah! [*He stops, chokes, and then stares wildly around him.*] Mamma. Mamma. [*He is having his first stroke.*]

Arnold Wesker, *Chicken Soup with Barley*

a) How old do you think Ada and Ronnie are?
b) Where do Ada and Ronnie live?
c) Why does Ada leave?
d) Who do you think Dave might be?
e) What difference in behaviour do you notice between Ada and Ronnie? Why do they react so differently?
f) Why does Sarah use the third person so much ('Him', 'my fine man', etc.)?
g) How would you describe the relationship between Harry and Sarah? Who seems the stronger?
h) Do you think Harry was 'the good, considerate father'?

3.2 Discuss the following points in class.
a) Do you agree with Ronnie that 'you can solve things by talking about them'? Or do you prefer Harry's reaction, 'Leave me alone'? In what ways is your opinion influenced by your own experience of family relationships?
b) 'What's a mother for?' asks Sarah. How has she interpreted her role, and why? What do *you* think a mother's for?

4.1 Text C 📼

The next passage also centres on a mother's role. As you read and listen to the scene, look for the similarities and differences between Sarah and Albert's mother.

ALBERT: Mr. Ryan's leaving. You know Ryan. He's leaving the firm. He's been there years. So Mr. King's giving a sort of party for him at his house . . . well, not exactly a party, not a party, just a few . . . you know . . . anyway, we're all invited. I've got to go. Everyone else is going. I've got to go. I don't want to go, but I've got to.
MOTHER [*bewildered, sitting*]: Well, I don't know . . .
ALBERT [*with his arm round her*]: I won't be late. I don't want to go. I'd much rather stay with you.
MOTHER: Would you?
ALBERT: You know I would. Who wants to go to Mr. King's party?
MOTHER: We were going to have our game of cards.
ALBERT: Well, we can't have our game of cards.
  [*Pause.*]
MOTHER: Put the bulb in Grandma's room, Albert.
ALBERT: I've told you I'm not going down to the cellar in my white shirt. There's no light in the cellar either. I'll be pitch black in five minutes, looking for those bulbs.
MOTHER: I told you to put a light in the cellar. I told you yesterday.
ALBERT: Well, I can't do it now.
MOTHER: If we had a light in the cellar you'd be able to see where those bulbs were. You don't expect me to go down to the cellar?
ALBERT: I don't know why we keep bulbs in the cellar!
  [*Pause.*]
MOTHER: Your father would turn in his grave if he heard you raise your voice to me. You're all I've got, Albert. I want you to remember that. I haven't got anyone else. I want you . . . I want you to bear that in mind.

≫→

ALBERT: I'm sorry . . . I raised my voice.

He goes to the door.

[*Mumbling.*] I've got to go.

MOTHER [*following*]: Albert!

ALBERT: What?

MOTHER: I want to ask you a question.

ALBERT: What?

MOTHER: Are you leading a clean life?

ALBERT: A clean life?

MOTHER: You're not leading an unclean life, are you?

ALBERT: What are you talking about?

MOTHER: You're not messing about with girls, are you?
   You're not going to go messing about with girls tonight?

ALBERT: Don't be so ridiculous.

MOTHER: Answer me, Albert. I'm your mother.

ALBERT: I don't know any girls.

MOTHER: If you're going to the firm's party, there'll be girls
   there, won't there? Girls from the office?

ALBERT: I don't like them, any of them.

MOTHER: You promise?

ALBERT: Promise what?

MOTHER: That . . . that you won't upset your father.

ALBERT: My father? How can I upset my father? You're
   always talking about upsetting people who are dead!

MOTHER: Oh, Albert, you don't know how you hurt me, you
   don't know the hurtful way you've got, speaking of your
   poor father like that.

ALBERT: But he is dead.

MOTHER: He's not! He's living! [*Touching her breast.*] In here!
   And this is his house!
   [*Pause.*]

ALBERT: Look, Mum, I won't be late . . . and I won't . . .

MOTHER: But what about your dinner? It's nearly ready.

ALBERT: Seeley and Kedge are waiting for me. I told you not
   to cook dinner this morning. [*He goes to the stairs.*] Just
   because you never listen . . .

He runs up the stairs and disappears.

Harold Pinter, *A Night Out*

a) How old do you think Albert is?
b) What kind of job does he have?
c) Who are Seeley and Kedge?

d) Does Albert often go out in the evenings?
e) Is the situation a familiar one for Albert?
f) Do you think Albert would 'rather stay with' his mother? If not, why does he say it?
g) Albert's mother uses different stages of emotional blackmail to try to make Albert stay at home – 'our game of cards' is the first. Can you trace the others? What is the climax of this?
h) Why is Albert's mother so possessive?

4.2 Stage directions

a) In the Pinter passage, why is the stage direction '*Pause*' important, especially the third time it occurs? Why do you think Albert's mother pauses at the lines 'I want you...I want you to bear that in mind', and 'That...that you won't upset your father'? Do you think she does so deliberately, or is she at a loss for words?

b) Look more carefully at the stage directions in the extracts from Wesker's *Chicken Soup with Barley* and Pinter's *A Night Out*. The directions have various functions; for example, they:
– describe tones of voice;
– suggest gesture to accompany or substitute dialogue;
– indicate movement from one part of the stage to another.

i) Put the various stage directions from both passages into these three categories.
ii) Are there any other categories?
iii) Does either of the two playwrights use any one of the categories to particular effect?
iv) What is different about the stage direction '*He is having his first stroke*' at the end of the Wesker passage?

4.3 Discuss the following in groups of three or four.
a) Would you react like any of the younger characters in the passages (Paul, Ada, Ronnie, Albert) if your family situation were similar?
b) What do you think they can do about their family lives? Should or could they simply leave home?
c) Is family life necessarily as troubled as those we have read about?

5.1 Text D 📼

Lastly, here is a description of a happy family. See if, even here, there are any small things which might lead to difficulties similar to those of the other families.

Mr and Mrs John Knightley, from having been longer than usual absent from Surrey, were exciting, of course, rather more than the usual interest. Till this year, every long vacation since their marriage had been divided between Hartfield and Donwell Abbey; but all the holidays of this autumn had been given to sea- 5
bathing for the children; and it was therefore many months since they had been seen in a regular way by their Surrey connections, or seen at all by Mr Woodhouse, who could not be induced to get so far as London, even for poor Isabella's sake; and who, consequently, was now most nervously and apprehensively happy in 10
forestalling this too short visit.

He thought much of the evils of the journey for her, and not a little of the fatigues of his own horses and coachman, who were to bring some of the party the last half of the way; but his alarms were needless: the sixteen miles being happily accomplished, and 15
Mr and Mrs John Knightley, their five children, and a competent number of nursery-maids, all reaching Hartfield in safety. The bustle and joy of such an arrival, the many to be talked to, welcomed, encouraged, and variously dispersed and disposed of, produced a noise and confusion which his nerves could not have 20
borne under any other cause; nor have endured much longer even for this; but the ways of Hartfield and the feelings of her father were so respected by Mrs John Knightley, that in spite of maternal solicitude for the immediate enjoyment of her little ones, and for their having instantly all the liberty and attendance, 25
all the eating and drinking, and sleeping and playing, which they could possibly wish for, without the smallest delay, the children were never allowed to be long a disturbance to him, either in themselves or in any restless attendance on them.

Mrs John Knightley was a pretty, elegant little woman, of 30
gentle, quiet manners, and a disposition remarkably amiable and affectionate, wrapped up in her family, a devoted wife, a doting mother, and so tenderly attached to her father and sister that, but for these higher ties, a warmer love might have seemed impossible. She could never see a fault in any of them. She was not a woman 35
of strong understanding or any quickness; and with this resem-
blance of her father, she inherited also much of his constitution; was delicate in her own health, over-careful of that of her children, had many fears and many nerves, and was as fond of her own Dr

Wingfield in town as her father could be of Dr Perry. They were ⁣40
alike, too, in a general benevolence of temper, and a strong habit
of regard for every old acquaintance.

Mr John Knightley was a tall, gentleman-like, and very clever
man, rising in his profession; domestic, and respectable in his
private character: but with reserved manners which prevented his ⁣45
being generally pleasing; and capable of being sometimes out of
humour. He was not an ill-tempered man, not so often unreason-
ably cross as to deserve such a reproach: but his temper was not
his great perfection; and, indeed, with such a worshipping wife, it
was hardly possible that any natural defects in it should not be ⁣50
increased. The extreme sweetness of her temper must hurt his.

Jane Austen, *Emma*

5.2 a) Write some notes on the small, seemingly insignificant things in the
passage which could lead to family difficulties. Then discuss them
with a partner. Does Jane Austen's way of writing about them make
it easy, or difficult, to identify them?

b) Write *two* paragraphs.
  – In the first, say which of all the family arrangements presented in
    the passages you would prefer to live in (if you *had* to make a
    choice!) and why.
  – In the second, give a brief description of your own family and say
    how it differs from, or is similar to, the ones you have read about.

6 Simulation

Work in groups of four or five.
You are a group of friends who have just left school, but you have been
unable to find jobs to your liking. All of you are interested in social
work and especially in the work of family advice centres, but you do
not know how to go about making this a career. You decide to write to
the local authority to ask for information on such careers locally.
a) Discuss and make notes on your own experiences of family
   problems.
b) Add to your notes the experiences that you have gained indirectly
   through reading. You may include texts in this unit, and other
   books you have read both in English and your native language.
c) Discuss the form and content of the letter, which is to be addressed
   to the Social Services Authority.   ⟫→

d) Write individual versions of the letter, compare them, and decide on the final version.

e) Show your letter to the other groups, and read theirs.

7 Dialogue

a) There are dialogues in the song, the Lawrence passage, and the plays.
   – How far do the characters really communicate through dialogue? Might dialogue sometimes be an *obstacle* to communication?
   – When is communication achieved without dialogue?

b) Work in pairs.
   There is no dialogue in the passage from *Emma*. What would a dialogue between Mr Woodhouse and his daughter on her safe arrival back be like? In your discussion, use especially the ideas you find in the second paragraph. Write notes, then compare your ideas with those of other pairs in the class.

POSTSCRIPT

All happy families resemble one another, each unhappy family is unhappy in its own way.

Leo Tolstoy, *Anna Karenina*

2 Environment

It isn't going to last.

1 Theme

Question
(Brazilian Government)

'These ecologists are
worrying about us
going in and chopping
down the Brazilian forest.
But why?
There is nothing there.'

Answer   (Pete Wilkinson, Friends of the Earth)

'A typical dogmatic view – that if an area contains no human life, then it's there to do
whatever you like with it. Nobody sees that there are other passengers on this planet
with us and they have a function to perform. And here we are preparing to chop the
whole lot down before properly finding out what that function is. It's just crazy.'

a) Is there any harm in chopping down a tree?
b) Do you know any areas which contain no human life? What life is
    there?
c) What in your view is the function of those aspects of life in the area
    you have described?
d) What is your own attitude to men changing the environment for
    their own convenience?
e) To Pete Wilkinson, 'chopping down the Brazilian forest' is a terrible
    tragedy. Working with a partner, see if you can work out what this
    tragedy means in terms of specific losses. Then read the statement of
    the problem given by the World Ecological Areas Programme,
    which follows, and discuss the points you did *not* think of.

World Ecological Areas Programme

A Proposal to save the World's Tropical Rain Forests.

1. The world's remaining tropical forests are being destroyed so fast that, at current trends, by the end of this century, only the most inaccessible will remain. This terrible tragedy will mean:

   – the destruction of the way of life of the indigenous peoples who inhabit these areas which must lead to their systematic pauperisation i.e. to their transformation into a marginal, largely unemployed proletariat leading a miserable and precarious existence in the shanty towns surrounding already drastically overcrowded cities:

   – the disappearance of a considerable proportion of the world's trees and plant species, many of which have not even been identified:

   – the disappearance in the wild of much of the world's remaining wildlife, including large cats such as the tiger and Clouded leopard and primates such as the gorilla and orang utan:

   – the loss of an inestimable reservoir of genetic resources that could be exploited to provide new foods, medicines, textiles, etc., and raw materials including bases for fuels

which could be of vital importance in a largely unforeseeable future:

   – soil erosion by wind and water – as most tropical soils have a low organic content and may become little more than dust, while others become brick-like laterite once they are deprived of their tree cover – in many cases leading to eventual desertification:

   – massively increased run-off to rivers and, in particular, when their beds have been raised following erosion from the mountains above, to floods in the surrounding plains – since only a fraction of the rainwater that can be stored around the root system of a tropical forest can be retained in the eroded soils of bare mountainsides:

   – reduced transpiration and hence precipitation, with a further reduction in water availability:

   – increase in the CO_2 released into the atmosphere but reduced absorption of CO_2 by depleted plant life with climatic consequences that are likely to be detrimental to world food production:

   – the loss of the soil's capacity to provide timber and other benefits on a more realistic but sustainable basis:

   – an aesthetic and scientific loss of unparalleled dimensions.

2. What, we might ask, will the countries who are cutting down their forests obtain in exchange? The answer is foreign currency largely to pay for imported consumer products that only a minority can afford and raw materials required for industrial development, which occurring as it must, in decreasingly propitious conditions, seem doomed to be short-lived.

The Ecologist

2.1 Text A 🖭

As you read and listen to the poem, try to decide when it might have
been written.

The poplars are felled;—farewell to the shade,
And the whispering sound of the cool colonnade!
The winds play no longer and sing in the leaves,
Nor Ouse on his bosom their image receives.

Twelve years have elapsed since I first took a view   5
Of my favourite field, and the bank where they grew;
And now in the grass behold they are laid,
And the tree is my seat, that once lent me a shade.

The blackbird has fled to another retreat,
Where the hazels afford him a screen from the heat,   10
And the scene where his melody charmed me before,
Resounds with his sweet-flowing ditty no more.

My fugitive years are all hasting away,
And I must ere long lie as lowly as they,
With a turf on my breast, and a stone at my head,   15
Ere another such grove shall arise in its stead.

'Tis a sight to engage me, if any thing can,
To muse on the perishing pleasures of man;
Though his life be a dream, his enjoyments, I see,
Have a being less durable even than he.   20

William Cowper, *The Poplar Field*

a) One clue to the period in which the poem was written is its vocabulary. The following words are no longer in common use. Find out
   when they were current.
   behold – ditty – ere (long) – hasting away – lowly – stead

b) Other words are still current, but their use in the poem is not. Use
   your dictionary to find out about their present-day meaning and
   use, and compare them with their meaning and use in the poem.
   colonnade – bosom – lent – afford – charmed – turf – arise –
   engage   ⟫→

c) Many of the sentence structures are typical of the poem's period, and are generally recognisable as 'poetic'. Comment on the following. What makes them different from contemporary English structures, and in what way are they poetic?
   – The winds play no longer and sing in the leaves
   – Nor Ouse on his bosom their image receives
   – And now in the grass behold they are laid
   – And the tree is my seat that once lent me a shade
   – Though his life be a dream, his enjoyments, I see,
     Have a being less durable even than he.

d) In thinking about more contemporary versions of the above sentences, were you forced, or tempted to change any of the words?

2.2 Cowper contrasts past and present. What language does he use to express the contrast? Talk about the past-present contrasts between the following:
a) row of poplar trees / cut down
b) their reflection in the water / nothing to see
c) sit under the trees / on them
d) the blackbirds singing / flown away
e) Cowper, strong and alive / die soon

2.3 a) Study the two pictures. They are of the same place, but one photograph was taken in 1974, and the other towards the end of the nineteenth century. Make some notes on the differences.

b) Work in groups of four, students A, B, C and D.
   Students A and B: Discuss and make notes on the advantages of
   living in the 20th century and the disadvantages of living in the
   19th century. Then discuss your findings with students C and D.
   Students C and D: Discuss and make notes on the advantages of
   living in the 19th century and the disadvantages of living in the
   20th century. Then discuss your findings with students A and B.

2.4 Write a letter to a friend about a place where there have been many
changes in the environment. If you do not know one, write about the
pictures above and opposite. Concentrate on specific losses.

3.1 Text B 📼

As you read and listen to this poem, what strikes you most —
differences, or similarities, between this poet's feelings and those of
Cowper?

I thought it would last my time—
The sense that, beyond the town,
There would always be fields and farms,
Where the village louts could climb
Such trees as were not cut down;   5
I knew there'd be false alarms

In the papers about old streets
And split-level shopping, but some
Have always been left so far;
And when the old part retreats   10
As the bleak high-risers come
We can always escape in the car.

Things are tougher than we are, just
As earth will always respond
However we mess it about;   15
Chuck filth in the sea, if you must:
The tides will be clean beyond.
—But what do I feel now? Doubt?

Or age, simply? The crowd
Is young in the M1 café;   20
Their kids are screaming for more—
More houses, more parking allowed,
More caravan sites, more pay.
On the Business Page, a score

Of spectacled grins approve   25
Some takeover bid that entails
Five per cent profit (and ten
Per cent more in the estuaries): move
Your works to the unspoilt dales
(Grey area grants)! And when   30

You try to get near the sea
In summer . . .
            It seems, just now,

To be happening so very fast;
Despite all the land left free   35
For the first time I feel somehow
That it isn't going to last,

That before I snuff it, the whole
Boiling will be bricked in
Except for the tourist parts—   40
First slum of Europe: a role
It won't be so hard to win,
With a cast of crooks and tarts.

And that will be England gone,
The shadows, the meadows, the lanes, 45
The guildhalls, the carved choirs.
There'll be books; it will linger on
In galleries; but all that remains
For us will be concrete and tyres.

Most things are never meant.   50
This won't be, most likely: but greeds
And garbage are too thick-strewn
To be swept up now, or invent
Excuses that make them all needs.
I just think it will happen, soon.   55

Philip Larkin, *Going, Going*

a) Discuss your general impressions of differences or similarities
   between Larkin's poem and Cowper's.

b) Some words and expressions make it clear that the poem is very
   modern. For example:
     split-level shopping
     bleak high-risers
     takeover bid
   Explain what you think these mean and then find other expressions
   in the poem which mean:
     an eating-place on the motorway
     the part of a newspaper dealing with finance
     a building development in very poor condition

3.2   The poem is full of images which use words in an unexpected way. Use
          your dictionary to find the meaning of:
            retreat – mess – snuff – boiling – cast   ⇉→

Then say what you think they mean in the contexts in which Larkin uses them:
a) ...when the old part retreats
   As the bleak high-risers come
b) However we mess it about
c) ...before I snuff it
d) ...the whole Boiling
e) ...a cast of crooks and tarts

3.3 Look again at *The Poplar Field* and see if you can find points where Cowper and Larkin are talking about very similar things. Compare and contrast what they say.
a) How do they each speak about the loss of natural countryside in the first two stanzas of each poem?
b) Larkin says 'Things are tougher than we are' (1.13). Does Cowper in his last stanza seem to agree or not?
c) What are the ways in which the poets mention their own deaths?
d) 'The unspoilt dales' and 'all the land left free' are both considered by Larkin to be threatened. By what? Do you find a similar sense of continuing threat to the landscape in Cowper? Or do you think he perhaps wants us to think of something more personal too?

3.4 a) Are Cowper and Larkin writing about the same problem? If so, what, in a few words, is the problem? If not, what do you think they are each writing about?
b) Larkin gives us a clearer picture of the whole country at the time of his writing. Do you think he has a reason for this? Is Cowper, for example, more concerned with himself and his life than with the destruction of nature?
c) By examining these contrasts, can you now find lines in both poems which you think show clearly (i) the similarities, (ii) the differences in intention of the two poets?
d) We have seen that Larkin uses expressions which could be termed 'colloquial' ('mess it about', for example). Find words and phrases in both poems which show the difference between Cowper's 'poetic' and Larkin's 'colloquial' language. 'Felled' might contrast with 'cut down', for example.
e) Do you think that one of the two poems is *more recognisably* a poem? What things contribute to this impression?
f) Do you find that the rhymes in one of the poems are more obvious than in the other? What is it, in your view, that makes them more obvious?

g) Larkin 'runs on' the lines of his poem; that is, he continues a sentence from one line to another sometimes. Do you feel the effect of this? You will have to *listen to* the poem at the same time as reading it in order to comment on this. Do you prefer the more ordered verses of Cowper, or the 'run on' style of Larkin? Do you feel that their different ways of writing in this respect are suited to the differences in their subject and/or their feelings and attitudes?

h) Why do you think Larkin stops after 'In summer...' (in the sixth stanza)? What do you think he could have gone on to say? Does Cowper also leave things unsaid? Why, or why not? The title *Going, Going* also leaves something unsaid. What and why?

4.1 Text C

Read this passage and make a note of those words which best express the author's feelings about man's destruction of the natural environment.

The farmer knows something that the whole of civilized mankind seems to have forgotten, namely, that the resources of life on our planet are not inexhaustible. In the United States it was only after wide expanses of ploughland had been turned into ⁵ desert through ruthless exploitation of the top soil, after large districts had been devastated by tree-felling, and countless useful animal species had become extinct that these facts gradually began to be realized again, mainly because many large ¹⁰ agricultural, fishing and whaling industries began to feel the effects financially. Nevertheless, the truth has only just began to penetrate to the consciousness of the general public . . .

When civilized man destroys in blind vandalism ¹⁵ the natural habitat surrounding and sustaining him he threatens himself with ecological ruin. Once he begins to feel this economically he will probably realize his mistakes, but by then it may be too late. Least of all does he notice how much this barbarian ²⁰ process damages his own mind . . .

How can one expect a sense of reverential awe for anything in the young when all they see around them is man-made and the cheapest and

⟫→

ugliest of its kind? For the city dweller, even his   25
view of the sky is obscured by the skyscrapers
and chemical clouding of the atmosphere. No
wonder the progress of civilization goes hand in
hand with the deplorable disfigurement of town
and country.   30

Konrad Lorenz, *Civilized Man's Eight Deadly Sins*

4.2   Konrad Lorenz believes that 'this barbarian process damages (man's)
own mind'. Do you think this is true? In what ways? Discuss this in
small groups, make notes and then report back to the class.

4.3   a) Which of the texts in this unit do you find most effective in terms of
the theme 'environment'? Do you prefer the poems to the prose text,
or vice versa? Why?
b) Who are the texts addressed to, do you think, and what seems to be
the writer's purpose in achieving communication? In this respect,
does Larkin seem to be nearer Cowper or Lorenz?

5 Simulation

You have decided to prepare a long-term plan to reverse negative
developments in the environment of the modern world.
a) Look through the passages in this unit and make a list of those
developments you would like to see reversed. Add any others that
are a matter of concern to you.
b) Compare your list with that of a partner and discuss any action that
could be taken to improve the situation.
c) The discussion. Draw up a plan covering:
   – immediate action;
   – the first three years;
   – the following ten years.
d) Follow-up. Write brief reports on the three plans you have decided
on.

6 Contrast

a) Look carefully again at texts A, B and C in this unit. They derive much of their effect from the *contrasts* that they express and there are many specific language items in them that convey these contrasts. An example is Cowper's use of expressions like 'no longer' and 'no more' in contrasting present and past. Make a list from the texts of other items which convey contrasts of various kinds.

b) Is ecology a problem in your country? What is, or is not, done, and what *should* be done about it? Write about this contrast in any one of the following forms:
   – a newspaper article;
   – a letter to an official body;
   – an opening address to a conference.

POSTSCRIPT

Men have an extraordinarily erroneous opinion of their position in nature, and the error is ineradicable.

W. Somerset Maugham, *A Writer's Notebook*

3 War

A very nasty outbreak of peace.

1.1 Theme

Read the extracts and make a note of the different attitudes to war, and reasons for going to war, that they show. Can you imagine someone wanting to go to war, or enjoying war?

Apart from Sudan, there was little else on offer. Rumours abounded that the CIA were hiring mercenaries for training anti-Communist Meos in Cambodia, and that some Persian Gulf sheikhs were getting fed up with their dependence on British military advisers and were looking for mercenaries who would be entirely their own dependents. The story was that there were jobs going for men prepared to fight for the sheikhs in the hinterland, or take charge of palace security. Shannon doubted all of these stories; for one thing he would trust the CIA like a hole in the head, and the Arabs were not much better when it came to making up their minds.

Outside of the Gulf, Cambodia and Sudan, there was little scope, and no good wars. In fact he foresaw in the offing a very nasty outbreak of peace.

Frederick Forsyth, *The Dogs of War*

– Do you think Shannon is being ironic or serious?
– Why does he consider peace would be nasty?
– What do you think a 'good war' would be for him?
– Would you like a job as a mercenary?
– What do you think of such professionals?

That war is an evil is something which we all know, and it would be pointless to go on cataloguing all the disadvantages involved in it. No one is forced into war by ignorance, nor, if he thinks he will gain from it, is he kept out of it by fear. The fact is that one side thinks that the profits to be won outweigh the risks to be incurred, and the other side is ready to face danger rather than accept an immediate loss.

Thucydides, *History IV 4*

Thucydides was writing at the time of the Peloponnesian War between the ancient Greek states of Athens and Sparta. Has war become in some way more complex since those times? Or is that perhaps a fallacy?

26

1.2 Work in small groups.
  a) Compare your notes on attitudes to war and reasons for going to war.
  b) Discuss your answers to the questions on *The Dogs of War* extract.
  c) Discuss whether you think the nature and/or manifestations of war have changed or not throughout the centuries.
  d) War is a subject often used for purposes of entertainment. Why is it, do you think, that we can laugh at it?

And why do so many of us seem to enjoy its horror?

Goscinny and Uderzo, *Asterix and the Chieftain's Shield*

2.1 Text A 📼

Read and listen to Henry V's exhortation to his army before the Battle
of Agincourt. What differences can you note between Henry's and
Shannon's attitudes to war?

Once more unto the breach, dear friends, once more,
Or close the wall up with our English dead.
In peace there's nothing so becomes a man
As modest stillness and humility:
But when the blast of war blows in our ears,   5
Then imitate the action of the tiger;
Stiffen the sinews, conjure up the blood,
Disguise fair nature with hard-favour'd rage;
Then lend the eye a terrible aspect;
Let it pry through the portage of the head   10
Like the brass cannon; let the brow o'erwhelm it

As fearfully as doth a gallèd rock
O'erhang and jutty his confounded base,
Swill'd with the wild and wasteful ocean.
Now set the teeth and stretch the nostril wide,   15
Hold hard the breath, and bend up every spirit
To his full height! On, on, you noblest English!
Whose blood is fet from fathers of war-proof;
Fathers that, like so many Alexanders,
Have in these parts from morn till even fought,   20
And sheath'd their swords for lack of argument.
Dishonour not your mothers; now attest
That those whom you call'd fathers did beget you.
Be copy now to men of grosser blood,
And teach them how to war. And you, good yeomen,   25
Whose limbs were made in England, show us here
The mettle of your pasture; let us swear
That you are worth your breeding; which I doubt not;
For there is none of you so mean and base
That hath not noble lustre in your eyes.   30
I see you stand like greyhounds in the slips,
Straining upon the start. The game's afoot:
Follow your spirit; and upon this charge
Cry, "God for Harry, England, and Saint George!"

William Shakespeare, *Henry V*

a) To make his exhortation effective, King Henry makes conscious
   appeal to sentiments he knows his men have. Find parts of his
   speech which appeal to sentiments connected with:
      manhood   parenthood   patriotism   pride   nobility
b) Pick out all the phrases which suggest physical action.
c) Pick out the *similes* in the speech. Are they suitable in the context?
d) After the reference to the tiger in line 6, there are two similes. When
   does the King return to the tiger reference?
e) The King tells his men to 'imitate the action of the tiger' (1.6), to
   'Disguise fair nature with hard-favour'd rage' (1.8), and yet calls
   them 'noblest English' of whom none is 'so mean and base, That
   hath not noble lustre in your eyes'. Do you find anything contra-
   dictory, inconsistent, or ironic in this?

2.2 Discuss the following in groups of three or four. Take notes on your
conclusions and share them with the rest of the class.
   a) Remember that this speech was written to be acted in a theatre.
      What do you think the audience's reaction to it would be?
   b) Would you fight for your country, or for your beliefs? What would
      motivate you to fight?
   c) Do you think it is possible to be neutral in time of war, if your own
      country is threatened?

3.1 **Text B**

As you read and listen to Wilfred Owen's sonnet, try to decide whose
point of view he is writing from. From the point of view of someone
who is personally and physically involved in the war, or from that of a
parent of one of the soldiers, a politician, or someone else?

What passing-bells for these who die as cattle?
   —Only the monstrous anger of the guns,
   Only the stuttering rifles' rapid rattle
Can patter out their hasty orisons.
No mockeries now for them; no prayers nor bells;   5
   Nor any voice of mourning save the choirs,—
The shrill, demented choirs of wailing shells;
   And bugles calling for them from sad shires.

What candles may be held to speed them all?
   Not in the hands of boys, but in their eyes   10
Shall shine the holy glimmers of good-byes.
   The pallor of girls' brows shall be their pall;
Their flowers the tenderness of patient minds,
And each slow dusk a drawing-down of blinds.

Wilfred Owen, *Anthem for Doomed Youth*

Work in pairs or small groups. Take *one* of the following questions for
each pair/group and discuss and take notes on possible answers.
Whichever part of the poem your question refers to – (c), for example,
refers only to one line – answer it with reference to *the poem as a whole.*
   a) The first eight lines contain many *sounds.* Note down the sound
      words. What kind of sounds do they indicate?
   b) What effect does the repetition of 'Only', 'No' and 'Nor' give?
   c) Where are the 'sad shires' (l.8)?

d) In the second part, sound gives way to light and shade. Note down the 'light' words. What are the colours of the light? How does the last line change the light?

e) Why does the poet mention choirs (ll.6 and 7) and candles (l.9)? What other suggestions of the same kind can you find in the poem?

f) Whose are the 'patient minds' (l.13)?

g) What effect does the use of rhyme have on the impact of the poem?

3.2 a) Now give your answers, as fully as possible, to the class as a whole.

b) Discuss possible answers to these questions:
   – Is the poet directly involved in the war, or not?
   – What war is he writing about, do you think?

4.1 Text C

In a similar situation, another two poets who wrote during the same war describe moments of joy. In what ways are the poems similar, and in what ways different? Which do you prefer?

Sombre the night is.
And though we have our lives, we know
What sinister threat lurks there.

Dragging these anguished limbs, we only know
This poison-blasted track opens on our camp—
On a little safe sleep.

But hark! joy—joy—strange joy.
Lo! heights of night ringing with unseen larks.
Music showering on our upturned list'ning faces.

Death could drop from the dark
As easily as song—
But song only dropped,
Like a blind man's dreams on the sand
By dangerous tides,
Like a girl's dark hair for she dreams no ruin lies there,
Or her kisses where a serpent hides.

Isaac Rosenberg, *Returning,
We Hear the Larks*

Everyone suddenly burst
    out singing;
And I was filled with such delight
As prisoned birds must find
    in freedom,
Winging wildly across the white
Orchards and dark-green
    fields; on—on—and
    out of sight.

Everyone's voice was
    suddenly lifted;
And beauty came like the
    setting sun:
My heart was shaken with
    tears; and horror
Drifted away. . . O, but
    Everyone
Was a bird; and the song
    was wordless; the
    singing will never be
    done.

Siegfried Sassoon, *Everyone Sang*

31

4.2 Look more closely at Rosenberg's poem.
- a) Almost all the adjectives in the poem describe the pain of war. What are the exceptions? Why are they concentrated in one part of the poem?
- b) Does the lark's song last long?
- c) What colours do you find in the poem?
- d) 'Dropped' refers to other things apart from song. What are they?

Look more closely at Sassoon's poem.
- e) Read the poem and listen to the recording at the same time. What is the effect of combinations of consonants and vowels, s – f – i – w for example? How do these effects relate to what the poet is attempting to communicate?
- f) The word 'Everyone' is used three times in the poem, and also in the title. Why? Why does the word have a capital E the third time it is used, in the middle of a line?
- g) The last lines of the first and second parts of the poem are longer than the others. Is there any reason for this, do you think?

4.3 a) Look at your notes on 1.2 (a) and (d) of this unit. Have you discovered any more ways of looking at war, since you read King Henry's speech and the poems?
- b) Most people would consider 'the horror of war' or, like Thucydides, 'the evil of war', as expressions close to their own sentiments. Much of what you have read in the texts of this unit illustrates, in one way or another, ways in which the horror and the evil can be kept at bay, distanced from ourselves, so that we do not feel the full painful effect. If you agree with this statement, discuss ways in which this is achieved.
- c) Think of a time when you suffered acutely, and how you tried to alleviate the pain. Write a short piece about the experience.
- d) Re-read the piece you have just written, and those of other students. Does anything in them suggest that you and they have attempted to distance yourselves from the experience?

5 Simulation 🔲

Listen to the speech made by Winston Churchill to the House of
Commons on 13th May 1940, during the Second World War. The text
is given below, but do not look at it until later.

You ask, What is our policy? I will say: It is to
wage war, by sea, land, and air, with all our might
and with all the strength that God can give us: to
wage war against a monstrous tyranny, never sur-
passed in the dark, lamentable catalogue of human
crime. That is our policy. You ask, What is our
aim? I can answer in one word: Victory – victory
at all costs, victory in spite of all terror; victory,
however long and hard the road may be: for
without victory there is no survival. Let that be
realised: no survival for the British Empire; no
survival for all that the British Empire has stood
for, no survival for the urge and impulse of the
ages, that mankind will move forward towards its
goal. But I take up my task with buoyancy and
hope. I feel sure that our cause will not be suffered
to fail among men. At this time I feel entitled to
claim the aid of all, and I say, 'Come, then, let us
go forward together with our united strength'.

Winston Churchill, Speech to the House of Commons, 13 May 1940

Imagine that this speech has been quoted by an acquaintance of yours,
a politician, in favour of fighting yet another war.
a) – If you are *not in agreement* with him, collect arguments *against*
      going to war from the texts in this unit.
    – If you *agree* with him, collect arguments *in favour of* going to war
      from the texts in this unit.
b) Add any literary references you can to support your argument, from
    literature in the English, your own or any other language.
c) Join the others in your class who are of your own opinion. Pool
    your literary references and develop an argument based on them.
    You might find yourselves all in one group, which will give your
    politician acquaintance some strong opposition!
d) – *Either* elect one person in each group to deliver the arguments as
      speeches.
    – *or* use the arguments you have prepared to debate the pros and
      cons of going to war.

33

6 Simile and metaphor

a) Look carefully again at the uses of figurative language, particularly simile and metaphor, in the texts of this unit and, if you wish, in other units you have read. Write down some examples. Can the ideas and feelings they communicate be expressed in any other, non-figurative way, and remain the *same* ideas and feelings?

b) What do you think of this cartoon?

Drawing by Koren; © 1979 The New Yorker Magazine, Inc.

c) Simile and metaphor are formal ways of expressing certain types of *association*. Any poem, for example, will contain a network of associations. Look at Wilfred Owen's poem on page 30. In the octet (the first 8 lines), there are associations between soldiers (the 'Doomed Youth') and cattle, between 'passing-bells' and 'guns', 'rifles', 'shells', and 'bugles', and again between 'shires' and 'cattle'. Can you work out this network of associations more fully?
Work out the network of associations in the sextet (the second part) and compare the octet with the sextet network. Which of these associations are conveyed in the form of simile and metaphor?

POSTSCRIPT

War is nothing more than the continuation of politics by other means.

Karl von Clausewitz, *On War*

4 Women

She could not have been 'a nice woman'.

1.1 Theme

A woman is a foreign land,
Of which, though there he settle young,
A man will ne'er quite understand
The customs, politics, and tongue.

Coventry Patmore, *The Angel in the House*

"Pontellier," said the Doctor, after a moment's reflection, "let your wife alone for a while. Don't bother her, and don't let her bother you. Woman, my dear friend, is a very peculiar and delicate organism – a sensitive and highly organized woman, such as I know Mrs Pontellier to be, is especially peculiar. It would require an inspired psychologist to deal successfully with them. . ."

Kate Chopin, *The Awakening*

a) What do these two attitudes indicate in the men who display them – superiority, fear, awe, lack of understanding, ignorance, or what? Is there, perhaps, an element of role playing?
b) Do you think Patmore is serious? Is he right? Do you think men and women have fixed attitudes to the other sex, or 'received', standard ideas about them, or judge the other sex in definite ways? See if the men and women in your class agree.
c) Does the Chopin quotation confirm or refute the Patmore lines, in your opinion?

1.2 a) Have you experienced any situations in which either of the sexes has been at a disadvantage *because* of their sex? Were the situations connected with work, or family, or social life, or what? Make some notes.
b) Talk with a partner about such situations. Have they had any influence on your attitudes to the opposite sex?

2.1 Text A

As you read this passage, try to decide what kind of man the speaker is (women may judge him differently from men). Also try to work out what the woman might do for a living.

I do not care for posturing women. But she *struck* me. I had to stop and look at her. The legs were well apart, the right foot boldly advanced, the left trailing with studied casual-ness. She held her right hand before her, almost touching the window, the fingers thrusting up like a beautiful 5
flower. The left hand she held a little behind her and seemed to push down playful lapdogs. Head well back, a faint smile, eyes half-closed with boredom or pleasure. I could not tell. Very artificial the whole thing, but then I am not a simple man. She was a beautiful woman. I saw her 10
most days, sometimes two or three times. And of course she struck other postures as the mood took her. Sometimes as I hurried by (I am a man in a hurry) I allowed myself a quick glance and she seemed to beckon me, to welcome me out of the cold. Other days I remember seeing her in 15
that tired, dejected passivity which fools mistake for femi-ninity.
  I began to take notice of the clothes she wore. She was a fashionable woman, naturally. In a sense it was her job. But she had none of the sexless, mincing stiffness of those 20

barely animated clothes-hangers who display *haute couture* in stuffy salons to the sound of execrable musak. No, she was another class of being. She did not exist merely to present a style, a current mode. She was above that, she was *beyond* that. Her clothes were peripheral to her beauty. 25 She would have looked good dressed in old paper bags. She disdained her clothes, she discarded them every day for others. Her beauty shone through those clothes . . . and yet they were beautiful clothes. It was autumn. She wore capes of deep russet browns, or twirling peasant skirts of 30 orange and green, or harsh trouser suits of burnt ochre. It was spring. She wore skirts of passion-fruit gingham, white calico shirts or lavish dresses of cerulean green and blue. Yes, I noticed her clothes, for she understood, as only the great portrait painters of the eighteenth century under- 35 stood, the sumptuous possibilities of fabric, the subtleties of folds, the nuance of crease and hem. Her body in its rippling changes of posture, adapted itself to the unique demands of each creation; with breathless grace the lines of her perfect body played tender counterpoint with the 40 shifting arabesques of sartorial artifice.

But I digress. I bore you with lyricism. The days came and passed. I saw her this day and not that, and perhaps twice on another day. Imperceptibly seeing her and not seeing her became a factor in my life, and then before I 45 knew it, it passed from factor to structure. Would I see her today? Would all my hours and minutes be redeemed? Would she look at me? Did she remember me from one time to another? Was there a future for us together . . . would I ever have the courage to approach her? Courage! 50 What did all my millions mean now, what now of my wisdom matured by the ravages of three marriages? I loved her . . . I wished to possess her. And to possess her it seemed I would have to buy her.

Ian McEwan, *Dead As They Come*

a) What ideas do the following words, taken together, give of both the man and the woman?
   posturing (l.1)   studied casualness (l.3)   thrusting up (l.5)
   playful lapdogs (l.7)   beckon (l.14)   mincing (l.20)
   Can you pick out other words and phrases which indicate attitudes or judgements?
b) Where is the 'lyricism' he bores us with (l.42)? Do you find it boring, attractive, revealing?

c) What aspects of the woman make her suitable for such a 'superior' man?

d) Are clothes 'peripheral to beauty' (l.25) usually?

e) What do you think he means by 'the sumptuous possibilities of fabric' (l.36)? Do you agree that it has such possibilities?

f) Do you think she has too many clothes? Does this give a clue as to her job?

g) Why does he need 'courage' (l.50)? Do you find it takes courage to make an approach to someone?

2.2   Work in pairs. By discussing with your partner, see if you can build up a character study of the man and the woman. Is it different from the impressions you had on first reading the passage?

Then share your ideas with the rest of the class, before your teacher reveals the woman's 'secret'. How does this new knowledge influence your reaction to the passage and your judgement of the characters?

3.1 Text B

In the town of Middlemarch Dorothea is also judged on the basis of limited information. As you read, note down reasons why she might be judged unfavourably. Also try to decide whether the author shares in the general judgement of Dorothea.

Dorothea herself had no dreams of being praised above other women, feeling that there was always something better which she might have done, if she had only been better and known better. Still, she never repented that she had given up position and fortune to marry Will Ladislaw, and he would have held   5
it the greatest shame as well as sorrow to him if she had repented. They were bound to each other by a love stronger than any impulses which could have marred it. No life would have been possible to Dorothea which was not filled with emotion, and she had now a life filled also with a beneficent   10
activity which she had not the doubtful pains of discovering and marking out for herself. Will became an ardent public man, working well in those times when reforms were begun with a young hopefulness of immediate good which has been much checked in our days, and getting at last returned to   15
Parliament by a constituency who paid his expenses. Dorothea could have liked nothing better, since wrongs existed, than that her husband should be in the thick of a struggle against

》》→

39

them, and that she should give him wifely help. Many who knew her, thought it a pity that so substantive and rare a 20 creature should have been absorbed into the life of another, and be only known in a certain circle as a wife and mother. But no one stated exactly what else that was in her power she ought rather to have done – not even Sir James Chettam, who went no further than the negative prescription that she ought not to 25 have married Will Ladislaw.

Sir James never ceased to regard Dorothea's second marriage as a mistake; and indeed this remained the tradition concerning it in Middlemarch, where she was spoken of to a younger generation as a fine girl who married a sickly 30 clergyman, old enough to be her father, and in little more than a year after his death gave up her estate to marry his cousin – young enough to have been his son, with no property, and not well-born. Those who had not seen anything of Dorothea usually observed that she could not have been 'a nice woman', 35 else she would not have married either the one or the other.

Certainly those determining acts of her life were not ideally beautiful. They were the mixed result of a young and noble impulse struggling amidst the conditions of an imperfect social state, in which great feelings will often take the aspect of 40 error, and great faith the aspect of illusion. For there is no creature whose inward being is so strong that it is not greatly determined by what lies outside it. A new Theresa will hardly have the opportunity of reforming a conventual life, any more than a new Antigone will spend her heroic piety in daring all 45 for the sake of a brother's burial: the medium in which their ardent deeds took shape is for ever gone. But we insignificant people with our daily words and acts are preparing the lives of many Dorotheas, some of which may present a far sadder sacrifice than that of the Dorothea whose story we know.   50

Her finely-touched spirit had still its fine issues, though they were not widely visible. Her full nature, like that river of which Cyrus broke the strength, spent itself in channels which had no great name on the earth. But the effect of her being on those around her was incalculably diffusive: for the growing 55 good of the world is partly dependent on unhistoric acts; and that things are not so ill with you and me as they might have been, is half owing to the number who lived faithfully a hidden life, and rest in unvisited tombs.

George Eliot, *Middlemarch*

a) Compare the positive and negative aspects of Dorothea which emerge from the passage. Decide who (the author / Sir James / other people) evaluates them positively or negatively. How do *you* evaluate them?

b) What do you think were 'those determining acts of her life' (l.37)?

c) The first sentence mentions 'something better' (l.2) which Dorothea never reached. Does the passage imply regret over this? If not, what compensates for her not having achieved something better?

d) What is the narrator's feeling about the opinion of 'many who knew her' (ll.19–20)?

e) What words tell us that Dorothea works for Will's 'struggle' (l.18) rather than her own? How does this connect with the general conclusions of the last two paragraphs?

f) Are the uses of 'ardent' different in lines 12 and 47?

g) Do you think George Eliot is judging society and/or Dorothea? What conclusions do you think she wants us to draw from what we have heard of Dorothea?

h) Does the passage seem to imply something about the role of women in the society of the period?

3.2 Re-read lines 37–41 of the George Eliot passage. Do they explain Dorothea's situation satisfactorily, in your opinion? In your own life, have you felt 'great feelings' or 'great faith' or something resembling them, which have had to be subdued to the demands of everyday life? Think about these things for a while, then discuss them with a partner before you recount your feelings to the class.

4.1 Text C

Emilia takes a very clear line about 'determining acts' in a woman's life. As you read, notice carefully who 'they' and 'we' (or 'us') refer to.

But I do think it is their husbands' faults
If wives do fall: say, that they slack their duties,
And pour our treasures into foreign laps;
Or else break out in peevish jealousies,
Throwing restraint upon us: or say they strike us,   5
Or scant our former having in despite,
Why, we have galls: and though we have some grace,
Yet have we some revenge. Let husbands know,
Their wives have sense like them: they see, and smell,
And have their palates both for sweet, and sour,   10

As husbands have. What is it that they do,
When they change us for others? Is it sport?
I think it is: and doth affection breed it?
I think it doth. Is't frailty that thus errs?
It is so too. And have not we affections?   15
Desires for sport? and frailty, as men have?
Then let them use us well: else let them know,
The ills we do, their ills instruct us so.

William Shakespeare, *Othello*

a) In lines 2 to 6 Emilia gives some examples of what men might do
   against women. Use your dictionary to check vocabulary you are
   not sure of, then say in your own words what these four crimes
   against women are.
b) Lines 2 to 6 are dominated by 'say'. How do lines 11 to 16 answer
   the affirmations in these lines?
c) Does Emilia's use of pronouns like 'they', which you noticed earlier,
   strengthen or weaken her argument?
d) Does the last line confirm or deny the first line?
e) Do you think Emilia's position is compatible with Coventry
   Patmore's?
f) Do you agree with Emilia?

4.2   Does the fact that Emilia is speaking aloud (in a play) make her
message any more or less forceful than George Eliot's? Try to pick out
some strengths in the Eliot passage which come from the presence of a
third-person narration, and compare them with the strengths and any
weaknesses you can find in Emilia's speech.

5 Text D

Read the passage to see how far it is true of the position of women in
your own country.

   The way our society is structured affects all human relationships.
Outside the home we have a system of power relationships:
worker/employer, individual/state, etc., and most people feel
powerless outside the home to a greater or lesser extent. People
can feel particularly powerless if their specific situation is beyond   5
their control: for example, if they are unemployed, scraping a
living, working at unpleasant jobs at unpleasant hours, or if they

have to 'be' people they don't want to be (such as a man 'having'
to be a breadwinner or a woman 'having' to be a housewife). The
resultant stresses and strains need outlets.   10

There are many different kinds of outlets. We can use our anger
or frustration by directing it constructively – into changing society.
But many people drown their feelings in drink, for example, or go
into a depression, or perhaps lash out. Many of us are inclined at
least sometimes to take out our frustration on people nearest us. 15
The limitations of private family life can act like a hot-house,
increasing frustration so that we lash out in our various ways.

The kind of destructive outlet that a woman uses may be
physical – either against her husband or children – but more
often it is psychological (against her family or herself). If the 20
violence is against the man, he still has the ultimate sanction: he
can walk out. The kind of oppressive violence a woman can
persistently use is more often directed towards her children –
because they cannot walk out. It is interesting that while the law
has protected children for some years, it is still equivocal in the 25
protection it gives to battered women. Commonly, women turn
violent feelings inwards: twice as many women as men suffer
from depression. Women who live in deprived areas, who don't
go to work, are, not surprisingly, the most vulnerable to depression.   30

As far as men are concerned, they have been brought up to use
their fists – and even encouraged to do so. It is not surprising,
therefore, that a man's outlet can, in its extreme form, involve
physical violence against his wife and family. Many women do
not have the ultimate sanction: we cannot easily leave home. 35
Men – even the most oppressed men – have a semblance of legal
and economic power in areas such as housing, employment,
education, child care, fertility control. Women are in comparison
relatively powerless. We would like to examine some of these
areas more closely.   40

In many marriages, the home is in the husband's name. If a
woman wants to leave home, she may find it very difficult to find
another one, because of prejudice against women in general or
against women with children in particular, or of course, because
she is on social security or very low pay. Furthermore, if a 45
woman leaves home with children, they are likely to be taken into
care – while she, on the other hand, is not considered 'homeless'.
After all, as the reasoning goes, she still has a home with her
husband! If she leaves home alone, she is even less likely to be
housed. Even if a woman is in the fortunate position of being able 50
to kick the man out of the home (and, even harder, keep him
out), she can still be held liable for her husband's rent arrears. So,
many battered women don't leave home because they can't.   ≫→

Women are also expected to look after children – even though we have no real choice about whether, when or in what circum- 55 stances we want them. Many women are consequently totally reliant on their husbands' incomes, or earn a pittance at part-time, low-paid jobs. Fathers, on the other hand, are not ulti- mately seen by society as responsible for the care of their children. A man can still drink all his earnings if he wishes. One of 60 the reasons some women put up with battering for so long is because they are concerned about how they could bring up the children with little money on their own if they left. Often, women finally leave only when they fear that their children are them- selves in physical or mental danger from their fathers. 65

Boston Women's Health Collective, *Our Bodies Ourselves*

a) How is this passage different from the others in this unit?
b) Can you make any connection between this passage and any of the others?
c) Is the passage more sympathetic to men or to women? Is it obvious that it was written by a woman?
d) Discuss in groups the possible injustices against women mentioned in the passage comparing them if you like with the acceptance of married life in the *Middlemarch* passage. Does this passage make you modify your ideas about Dorothea or Emilia?
e) Do the men and women in the class react differently to this passage? Why / why not?

6 Simulation

Here are some extracts from the British Press which reflect some twentieth-century attitudes to women, sexual discrimination and men-women relationships.
Imagine that Coventry Patmore, the Doctor in *The Awakening*, the first-person narrator of *Dead As They Come*, Dorothea, Emilia, and the author of *Our Bodies Ourselves* come together to discuss their reactions to these texts.
Work in groups of six, each of you adopting the views of one of the authors/characters. Re-read the passages to remind yourself clearly of their views and attitudes.
When you have expressed your reactions and discussed them, each write a short letter to *The Times* giving your view of any one of the texts.

SEX DISCRIMINATION ACT, 1975

No job advertisement which indicates or can reasonably be understood as indicating an intention to discriminate on ground of sex (eg by inviting applications only from males or only from females) may be accepted, unless:

1. The job is for the purpose of a private household; or
2. It is a business employing fewer than six persons; or
3. It is otherwise excepted from the requirements of the Sex Discrimination Act.

A statement must be made at the time the advertisement is placed saying which of the exceptions in the Act is considered to apply.

In addition to employment, the principal areas covered by the section of the Act which deals with advertisements are education, the supply of goods and services and the sale or letting of property.

It is the responsibility of advertisers to ensure that advertisement content does not discriminate under the terms of the Sex Discrimination Act.

"But are you going to be faithful to us?"

As today's bride walks down the aisle with her future husband, she has every excuse for being nervous. She is about to exchange vows of lifelong commitment, fidelity and mutual support. Yet all around her, she can see that many people do not and cannot live up to these vows. Her own marriage faces a one in three chance of divorce, if present trends continue.

Traditional marriage in Britain is currently in a turmoil. Not only is the divorce rate rising, but the rate at which people marry is falling. Living together is more popular than ever before. The shape of the family is now no longer one man, one woman and their children. Instead, there are growing numbers of families which include step-parents, half sisters and brothers, or merely one lone parent coping on her own.

Compared with other countries, Britain is still conservative in its marriage patterns. In America, the divorce rate is even more startling. Two out of five marriages end in divorce. In Sweden living together is now more popular than marriage among couples in their early twenties and a similar pattern seems to be emerging in Denmark.

Although this is happening on a smaller scale in Britain, it has not yet become such a marked trend. But if we do follow the American and Scandinavian patterns, the future will see many more couples living together before marriage – and even more divorce.

Interestingly enough, it is women rather than men who get a divorce in the courts. Seven out of ten divorces are granted to the wife. Divorce, of course, only reflects the legal winding up of a marriage which may have effectively broken up long before. The partner who petitions for divorce may not be the partner who broke up the marriage. Women usually have more to gain from the courts in the way of alimony, rights to the home, and child maintenance. But there is also a fascinating disproportion in one of the grounds that the sexes choose for divorce. The grounds of unreasonable or cruel behaviour are overwhelmingly chosen by ten times more women than men. Does this mean that women will put up with less than they used to?

Money and divorce: the new battle

THE BILL, due for its second reading in the House of Lords later this month, recognises the equality between man and wife by ending her right to maintenance after the breakdown of marriage.

Men will still be required to provide some sort of support to their offspring but, after a short interval in which the wife (who may not have worked for years) pulls herself together, maintenance to her can be stopped at the court's discretion. (The Bill does not say *who* should maintain child carers. Perhaps they feel that children should be more independent too and organise self-care groups.)

This concern for equality when marriage ends is not to be extended to the sanctified institution itself. In spite of recent rumblings, women will still be dependants under tax, social security, and pension laws.

The assumption that men will work and women will be mothers has left an indelible stamp on the organisation of employment: women in low-paying jobs which are easily abandoned, and men in higher-paying, career-structured, ones supported by caring wives at home. Women who leave work temporarily usually move even further down the skill and wage

The Matrimonial and Family Proceedings Bill is surrounded by controversy: Angela Phillips sees the pitfalls for women.

scale. The earnings gap grows wider.

To suggest then that many women emerge from marriage on equal terms with their partners is nonsense. Those few who do so will, in any case, find that the law takes that into account in any settlement. For the rest, this Bill abolishes any right to compensation for sacrifices made in the performance of those wifely duties that society still expects.

Not that ex-wives get much compensation now. The vast majority will be financially unaffected by this Bill because they get so little maintenance. Nothing minus nothing still equals nothing.

Studies show that 90 per cent

of maintenance orders (including child support) are for less than £20 per week and that over 50 per cent are for less than £5. In fact, second families (whom the Bill seeks to protect) are usually better off than the poverty-stricken one-parent families left behind. The non-earning, childless, alimony drone living on a lifetime's meal ticket is so hard to find that Campaign for Justice in Divorce (the driving force behind the Bill) is hard put to come up with an example for the BBC's World at One.

The Bill's clear message to women contemplating matrimony is: "Hang on to your job, just in case you cannot hang on to your man."

Meal ticket

THE Bill's critics (including lawyers from the Legal Action Group) point out:

● No employer could expect to impose contract terms like those which this Bill will force on the full-time housewife.

● Although children from this marriage would be supported until 18, their mother could be expected to support herself several years before that.

● The idea of a guilty party is being revived, which could leave the housewife without maintenance or home – as test cases have already established.

7 Sexist language

a) In recent years many people have taken objection to what is called sexist language: 'he' is often used to mean 'everyone', 'man' to mean 'mankind' (i.e. men and women) – even 'men and women' puts men first; why not 'women and men'? Look back through the book and see what similarly sexist attitudes you can find.

b) Objection has been taken to words like 'spokesman' and 'chairman' – do you prefer 'spokesperson' and 'chairperson'? And what about 'personipulate' instead of 'manipulate', 'herstory' instead of 'history', 'Personchester' instead of 'Manchester'? Are they only good for a modern laugh, or is there something serious behind them? Why do you think these questions have arisen in recent years? What should we do about them – adopt new forms, such as Ms instead of Mrs or Miss, or keep to the old ways? Is there any alternative to 'he/she' which is less cumbersome?

c) Are there areas which have predominantly masculine or feminine language? Talk in groups about one of the following and try to analyse how 'masculine' or 'feminine' the language you use is: football, child care, war, cooking, cars, love, ships, trade unions, teachers. Do you agree that 'the English language does indeed assume everybody to be male unless they are proved otherwise'? (Angela Carter, 'The Language of Sisterhood')

d) Sometimes sexist words are used in an insulting way. Women have been considered 'the weaker sex' (William Alexander), 'the lesser man' (Tennyson), and effeminacy has been considered a fault in men, just as mannishness has been thought of as a fault in women. Write a couple of paragraphs about attitudes of men to women and women to men, or about effeminacy and mannishness. Then compare the amount of sexist language you have used with the rest of the class.

POSTSCRIPT

What vain unnecessary things are men.
How well we do without 'em.

John Wilmot, Earl of Rochester, *Draft of a Satire on Man*

5 Authority

That is how we tell whether or not we live in a free country.

1 Theme

The LAW of the LORD

God spake all these words, saying,

I am the LORD thy God . . .

1. Thou shalt have no other gods before me.

2. Thou shalt not make unto thee any graven image, or any likeness of any thing that is in heaven above, or that is in the earth beneath, or that is in the water under the earth:

Thou shalt not bow down thyself to them, nor serve them: for I the LORD thy God am a jealous God, visiting the iniquity of the fathers upon the children unto the third and fourth generation of them that hate me; and shewing mercy unto thousands of them that love me, and keep my commandments.

3. Thou shalt not take the name of the LORD thy God in vain; for the LORD will not hold him guiltless that taketh His name in vain.

4. Remember the sabbath day to keep it holy. Six days shalt thou labour, and do all thy work: but the seventh day is the sabbath of the LORD thy God: in it thou shalt not do any work, thou, nor thy son, nor thy daughter, thy manservant, nor thy maidservant, nor thy cattle, nor thy stranger that is within thy gates:

For in six days the LORD made heaven and earth, the sea, and all that in them is, and rested the seventh day: wherefore the LORD blessed the sabbath day and hallowed it.

5. Honour thy father and thy mother: that thy days may be long upon the land which the LORD thy God giveth thee.

6. Thou shalt not kill.

7. Thou shalt not commit adultery.

8. Thou shalt not steal.

9. Thou shalt not bear false witness against thy neighbour.

10. Thou shalt not covet thy neighbour's house, thou shalt not covet thy neighbour's wife, nor his manservant, nor his maidservant, nor his ox, nor his ass, nor any thing that is thy neighbour's.

Exodus 20. 1-17.

The measure of a person's political authority is the taboos he can impose, and they can be rendered invalid and overruled only by the taboo of a higher official; this is the only limitation of function.

Franz Steiner, *Taboo*

48

a) Bear in mind the quotation from Steiner's *Taboo* as you do the
   following.
   – In the photograph, Mussolini is orating on the Capitoline Hill in
     Rome. Almost never did photographs show the footstool he liked
     to stand on for public speeches, but you can see it here. Make a list
     of all the things in the photograph which contribute to the
     assertion of authority.
   – What characteristics of the language of the Ten Commandments
     give them their authoritative tone?

b) Work in groups of four or five and discuss your work on (a) above.
   Then discuss the following.
   – We begin to experience the effects of authority from birth, and
     part of childhood consists of taboos imposed by well-meaning
     parents. Do such taboos represent a kind of aggression or do they
     act as guidelines that the child cannot do without?
   – Many child psychologists see the expression of the well-meaning
     parent's authority as a kind of aggression, a negative rather than a
     positive influence. Some common expressions of *verbal aggression*
     are warnings like the following:
       'You'll catch a cold.'
       'Are you sure you're wrapped up warm?'
       'You'll fall!'
       'I don't really like that friend of yours.'
     Try to remember some of the expressions of verbal aggression that
     were used on you when you were a child.
   – *Non-verbal* expressions of parental authority are used especially
     in infancy. Here are some examples, from the child's point of view:
       Being put to bed when you're not sleepy.
       Having your hand slapped when you're trying to get hold of
       something attractive.
       Having a dummy forced into your mouth when you're angry
       or hungry.
       Being forced to sit on the potty for hours on end.
     How many more can you think of?
   – What are the different types of authority that we have to learn to
     accept? In what ways have you attempted to react against them,
     and perhaps to impose your own authority?

2.1 Text A

As you read the passage, try to work out what the Hatter has done wrong, if anything.

'Give your evidence,' said the King; 'and don't be nervous, or I'll have you executed on the spot.'

This did not seem to encourage the witness at all: he kept shifting from one foot to the other, looking uneasily at the Queen, and in his confusion he bit a large piece out of his teacup instead 5 of the bread-and-butter.

Just at this moment Alice felt a very curious sensation, which puzzled her a good deal until she made out what it was: she was beginning to grow larger again, and she thought at first she would get up and leave the court; but on second thoughts she decided to 10 remain where she was as long as there was room for her.

'I wish you wouldn't squeeze so,' said the Dormouse, who was sitting next to her. 'I can hardly breathe.'

'I can't help it,' said Alice very meekly: 'I'm growing.'

'You've no right to grow *here*,' said the Dormouse. 15

'Don't talk nonsense,' said Alice more boldly: 'you know you're growing too.'

'Yes, but *I* grow at a reasonable pace,' said the Dormouse: 'not in that ridiculous fashion.' And he got up very sulkily and crossed over to the other side of the court. 20

All this time the Queen had never left off staring at the Hatter, and, just as the Dormouse crossed the court, she said to one of the officers of the court, 'Bring me the list of the singers in the last concert!' on which the wretched Hatter trembled so, that he shook both his shoes off. 25

'Give your evidence,' the King repeated angrily, 'or I'll have you executed, whether you're nervous or not.'

'I'm a poor man, your Majesty,' the Hatter began, in a trembling voice, '— and I hadn't begun my tea — not above a week or so — and what with the bread-and-butter getting so thin — and 30 the twinkling of the tea ——'

'The twinkling of the *what*?' said the King.

'It *began* with the tea,' the Hatter replied.

'Of course twinkling begins with a T!' said the King sharply. 'Do you take me for a dunce? Go on!' 35

'I'm a poor man,' the Hatter went on, 'and most things twinkled after that — only the March Hare said ——'

'I didn't!' the March Hare interrupted in a great hurry.

'You did!' said the Hatter.

'I deny it!' said the March Hare.   40

'He denies it,' said the King: 'leave out that part.'

'Well, at any rate, the Dormouse said ——' the Hatter went on, looking anxiously round to see if he would deny it too: but the Dormouse denied nothing, being fast asleep.

'After that,' continued the Hatter, 'I cut some more bread-and-   45
butter ——'

'But what did the Dormouse say?' one of the jury asked.

'That I can't remember,' said the Hatter.

'You *must* remember,' remarked the King, 'or I'll have you executed.'   50

The miserable Hatter dropped his teacup and bread-and-butter, and went down on one knee. 'I'm a poor man, your Majesty,' he began.

'You're a *very* poor *speaker*,' said the King.

Here one of the guinea-pigs cheered, and was immediately   55
suppressed by the officers of the court. (As that is rather a hard word, I will just explain to you how it was done. They had a large canvas bag which tied up at the mouth with strings: into this they slipped the guinea-pig, head first, and then sat upon it.)

'I'm glad I've seen that done,' thought Alice. 'I've so often read   60
in the newspapers, at the end of trials, "There was some attempt at applause, which was immediately suppressed by the officers of the court," and I never understood what it meant till now.'

'If that's all you know about it, you may stand down,' continued the King.   65   ⟫→

51

'I can't go no lower,' said the Hatter: 'I'm on the floor, as it is.'

'Then you may *sit* down,' the King replied.

Here the other guinea-pig cheered, and was suppressed.

'Come, that finishes the guinea-pigs!' thought Alice. 'Now we
shall get on better.'   70

'I'd rather finish my tea,' said the Hatter, with an anxious look
at the Queen, who was reading the list of singers.

'You may go,' said the King; and the Hatter hurriedly left the
court, without even waiting to put his shoes on.

'— and just take his head off outside,' the Queen added to one   75
of the officers; but the Hatter was out of sight before the officer
could get to the door.

Lewis Carroll, *Alice in Wonderland*

a) Why is the Hatter nervous?
b) The Hatter tries to report comments by the March Hare and the
   Dormouse. Did they really say anything?
c) Why are the two guinea-pigs 'suppressed'?
d) What impression do you have of the King and Queen?
e) Do you think the Hatter has any important 'evidence' to give?
f) Do you think the King and Queen really mean to have the Hatter
   executed?

2.2 a) In the passage from *Alice in Wonderland*, there is a great deal of
          wordplay which satirises the kind of authority which is so often a
          part of real-life formal situations – court hearings, in this case.
          Identify some examples and discuss what you think Lewis Carroll's
          attitude to authority might be.
       b) In the passage, the relationships that normally hold between
          question and answer, statement and response, are sometimes absent
          or changed in some way. What is the effect of this? Does it happen
          in real life?

2.3 Prepare a reading aloud of the Lewis Carroll passage so as to bring out
       the absurdity of the court's and the King's authority. You could work
       in groups of seven and play the following parts:
       Narrator / King / Queen / Hatter / March Hare / Member of the Jury /
       Alice.

2.4 Teachers / priests / policemen / entertainers / chairpersons.
All of these exercise authority in one way or another.

a) What is it about their appearance and general behaviour which enables them to convey this authority?

b) What are the characteristics of the language they use, and the way they use it? Give examples from your experience.

c) In their use of language, in what ways do they interact with those over whom they have authority? Do they differ much from individual to individual?

3.1 Text B 📼

How would you react if you found yourself in the situation described in this passage? What would you *feel, think* and *do*?

Outside, even through the shut window-pane, the world looked cold. Down in the street little eddies of wind were whirling dust and torn paper into spirals, and though the sun was shining and the sky a harsh blue, there seemed to be no colour in anything, except the posters that were plastered 5
everywhere. The black-moustachio'd face gazed down from every commanding corner. There was one on the house-front immediately opposite. BIG BROTHER IS WATCHING YOU, the caption said, while the dark eyes looked deep into Winston's own. Down at street level another poster, torn at one corner, flapped 10
fitfully in the wind, alternately covering and uncovering the single word INGSOC. In the far distance a helicopter skimmed down between the roofs, hovered for an instant like a blue-bottle, and darted away again with a curving flight. It was the police patrol, snooping into people's windows. The patrols did 15
not matter, however. Only the Thought Police mattered.

Behind Winston's back the voice from the telescreen was still babbling away about pig-iron and the overfulfilment of the Ninth Three-Year Plan. The telescreen received and transmitted simultaneously. Any sound that Winston made, above the level 20
of a very low whisper, would be picked up by it, moreover, so long as he remained within the field of vision which the metal plaque commanded, he could be seen as well as heard. There was of course no way of knowing whether you were being watched at any given moment. How often, or on what system, 25
the Thought Police plugged in on any individual wire was guesswork. It was even conceivable that they watched every-

body all the time. But at any rate they could plug in your wire
whenever they wanted to. You had to live – did live, from habit
that became instinct – in the assumption that every sound you   30
made was overheard, and, except in darkness, every movement
scrutinized.

George Orwell, *Nineteen Eighty-Four*

a) What are the Thought Police?
b) Who is Big Brother?
c) What is the effect on Winston of the ever-present watching
   authority?
d) Note down words and phrases that Orwell uses to create an
   atmosphere of insecurity and unfriendliness.
e) Words like 'snooping' (l.15) and 'babbling' (l.18) tell us something
   about Winston's attitude to authority. How do you think he feels
   about it?
f) Given Winston's attitude, what courses of action are open to him?
   In such a situation, would *your* attitude be any different? If so, what
   action would you take?

3.2 Work in groups of three or four. Does the kind of society that Orwell
describes bear any relation to reality, or do you find it an exaggerated
fantasy? Make notes, then exchange ideas.

4 Text C 📼

As you read this passage, look for all the information that will enable
you to make a list of all the characters in order of importance in the
hierarchy of authority.

Like all the other officers at Group Headquarters except Major Danby,
Colonel Cathcart was infused with the democratic spirit: he believed that all
men were created equal, and he therefore spurned all men outside Group
Headquarters with equal fervor. Nevertheless, he believed in his men. As he
told them frequently in the briefing room, he believed they were at least ten   5
missions better than any other outfit and felt that any who did not share this
confidence he had placed in them could get the hell out. The only way they
could get the hell out, though, as Yossarian learned when he flew to visit ex-
P.F.C. Wintergreen, was by flying the extra ten missions.
    "I still don't get it," Yossarian protested. "Is Doc Daneeka right or isn't   10
he?"

"How many did he say?"

"Forty."

"Daneeka was telling the truth," ex-P.F.C. Wintergreen admitted. "Forty missions is all you have to fly as far as Twenty-seventh Air Force Head- 15 quarters is concerned."

Yossarian was jubilant. "Then I can go home, right? I've got forty-eight."

"No, you can't go home," ex-P.F.C. Wintergreen corrected him. "Are you crazy or something?"

"Why not?" 20

"Catch-22."

"Catch-22?" Yossarian was stunned. "What the hell has Catch-22 got to do with it?"

"Catch-22," Doc Daneeka answered patiently, when Hungry Joe had flown Yossarian back to Pianosa, "says you've always got to do what your 25 commanding officer tells you to."

"But Twenty-seventh Air Force says I can go home with forty missions."

"But they don't say you have to go home. And regulations do say you have to obey every order. That's the catch. Even if the colonel were disobeying a Twenty-seventh Air Force order by making you fly more missions, you'd still 30 have to fly them, or you'd be guilty of disobeying an order of his. And then Twenty-seventh Air Force Headquarters would really jump on you."

Yossarian slumped with disappointment. "Then I really have to fly the fifty missions, don't I?" he grieved.

"The fifty-five," Doc Daneeka corrected him. 35

"What fifty-five?"

"The fifty-five missions the colonel now wants all of you to fly."

Hungry Joe heaved a huge sigh of relief when he heard Doc Daneeka and broke into a grin. Yossarian grabbed Hungry Joe by the neck and made him fly them both right back to ex-P.F.C. Wintergreen. 40

"What would they do to me," he asked in confidential tones, "if I refused to fly them?"

"We'd probably shoot you," ex-P.F.C. Wintergreen replied.

"*We*?" Yossarian cried in surprise. "What do you mean, *we*? Since when are you on their side?" 45

"If you're going to be shot, whose side do you expect me to be on?" ex-P.F.C. Wintergreen retorted.

Yossarian winced. Colonel Cathcart had raised him again.

Joseph Heller, *Catch-22*

a) How many missions will Yossarian have to fly?

b) Sum up the whole situation in a few words, like this:

> Yossarian wants...
>
> But Colonel Cathcart wants...
>
> Twenty-seventh Air Force Headquarters allows...
>
> But Colonel Cathcart...
>
> So Yossarian...

c) What is Catch-22? ⟫→

d) What impression does the passage give you of Colonel Cathcart?
e) What differences can you point out between the authority of Big Brother and the authority of Colonel Cathcart?
f) How often do they fly back and forward in the passage? Does all this movement add to the atmosphere?
g) Why does ex-P.F.C. Wintergreen change in his behaviour towards Yossarian? What can Yossarian do about it?
h) The tone of this passage is very different from that of the Orwell passage. Note down words and phrases that show Heller's irony and humour.
i) 'Raised' is a poker term indicating a challenge to which the opponent has to rise, or else admit defeat. What makes the term meaningful and appropriate here?

5 Text D 🖭

Now that you have been reading, thinking and talking for some time about authority, freedom, intrusions on privacy and related matters, see how you think Truscott, in Joe Orton's *Loot*, exercises his authority. How does he show his aggression? As you read the passage, try to decide:
– if Truscott is really from the Water Board
– if a crime has been committed
– if Hal is telling the truth
– where the scene is taking place
– why the money might be in church
– who Fay is

TRUSCOTT. But he is stupid. He's just admitted it. He must be the stupidest criminal in England. Unless – (*He regards* HAL *with mounting suspicion.*) – unless he's the cleverest. What was your motive in confessing to the bank job?
HAL. To prove I'm stupid.
TRUSCOTT. But you've proved the opposite.
HAL. Yes.
TRUSCOTT (*baffled, gnawing his lip*). There's more to this than meets the eye. I'm tempted to believe that you did have a hand in the bank job. Yes. I shall inform my superior officer. He will take whatever steps he thinks fit. I may be required to make an arrest.
FAY. The water board can't arrest people.
TRUSCOTT. They can in certain circumstances.
FAY. What circumstances?
TRUSCOTT. I'm not prepared to reveal the inner secrets of the

water board to a member of the general public. (*To* HAL.) Where's the money?

HAL (*closing his eyes, taking a deep breath*). It's being buried.

TRUSCOTT. Who's burying it?

HAL. Father Jellicoe, S.J.

TRUSCOTT. Come here! Come here!

> HAL *goes over, his hands trembling as they button up his coat.*

I'm going to ask you a question or two. I want sensible answers. None of your piss-taking. Is that understood? Do I make myself plain? I'm talking English. Do you understand?

HAL. Yes.

TRUSCOTT. All right then. As long as we know.

> *A pause, in which he studies* HAL.

Now, be sensible. Where's the money?

> HAL *looks at his watch.*

HAL. By now I'd say it was half-way up the aisle of the Church of St Barnabas and St Jude.

> *He half turns away.* TRUSCOTT *brings his fist down on the back of* HAL's *neck.* HAL *cries out in pain and collapses on to the floor rubbing his shoulder.*

FAY (*indignant*). How dare you! He's only a boy.

TRUSCOTT. I'm not impressed by his sex, miss (*To* HAL.) I asked for the truth.

HAL. I'm telling the truth.

TRUSCOTT. Understand this, lad. You can't get away with cheek. Kids nowadays treat any kind of authority as a challenge. We'll challenge you. If you oppose me in my duty, I'll kick those teeth through the back of your head. Is that clear?

HAL. Yes.

> *Door chimes.*

FAY. Would you excuse me, Inspector?

TRUSCOTT (*wiping his brow*). You're at liberty to answer your own doorbell, miss. That is how we tell whether or not we live in a free country.

> FAY *goes off left.*

(*Standing over* HAL.) Where's the money?

HAL. In church.

>TRUSCOTT *kicks* HAL *violently.* HAL *cries out in terror and pain.*

TRUSCOTT. Don't lie to me!
HAL. I'm not lying! It's in church!
TRUSCOTT (*shouting, knocking* HAL *to the floor*). Under any other
   political system I'd have you on the floor in tears!
HAL (*crying*). You've got me on the floor in tears.
TRUSCOTT. Where's the money?

Joe Orton, *Loot*

a) If we know that Truscott is really a police officer, does the effect of
   the passage change?
b) Why does he get so angry? What has it got to do with his authority?
c) Despite Truscott's attack on Hal, there is quite a lot of humour in
   the passage. For example:
   T: What was your motive in confessing to the bank job?
   H: To prove I'm stupid.
   T: But you've proved the opposite.
   H: Yes.
   What makes it funny?
d) Much of the humour of the extract from *Alice in Wonderland* is
   based on the Hatter's nervousness. Is Hal nervous for the same
   reasons? How similar is Hal's situation to the Hatter's? Is there any
   similarity between the King and Queen and Truscott?
e) Invent a story in which Hal would be telling the truth: that some
   stolen money is being buried by a priest. The following questions
   might help.
   What does a priest normally bury?
   In that case, what is the money in?
   Where are the usual contents of the coffin (i.e. the body)?
   How did it all happen?
   Does the priest know the coffin contains money?

6 Simulation

SITUATION
Imagine that the books from which the four extracts in this unit are
taken are not fictional. But times have changed and the King (*Alice in
Wonderland*), Big Brother (*Nineteen Eighty-Four*), Colonel Cathcart

(*Catch-22*) and Truscott (*Loot*) are to be brought to trial for the parts they have played in unjust societies.

ROLES AND PRELIMINARY TASKS
The Hatter, Winston, Yossarian, Hal: Draw up the evidence against your oppressors by making notes on the extracts in which you and they appear. At the trial, you will base your accusations on these notes.

The King, Big Brother, Colonel Cathcart, Truscott: Prepare your defence.

The Judge: Study the details of the case by re-reading the extracts.

The Jury (all other members of the class): Study the details of the case by re-reading the extracts.

SIMULATION
The trials.
a) Form four groups as follows:
   i)   The Hatter, the King, 2 or 3 jury members.
   ii) Winston, Big Brother, 2 or 3 jury members.
   iii) Yossarian, Colonel Cathcart, 2 or 3 jury members.
   iv) Hal, Truscott, 2 or 3 jury members.
   The juries will decide on individual sentences or acquittals. The Judge will move from group to group, following the development of each trial.
b) Report the results of your trial to the other groups and to the Judge, who will give approval or not as he thinks best.

7 Style

The various authors' attitudes are reflected in the *styles* they use – the special ways in which they use language. The situation of *Catch-22* is conveyed with sophisticated irony, that of *Nineteen Eighty-Four* with a grim sense of reality. Discuss ways you can characterise the other passages: the Ten Commandments, Steiner, Lewis Carroll, Joe Orton.

POSTSCRIPT

A dog's obeyed in office.

William Shakespeare, *King Lear*

6 Indifference

I am— yet what I am none cares or knows.

1 Theme

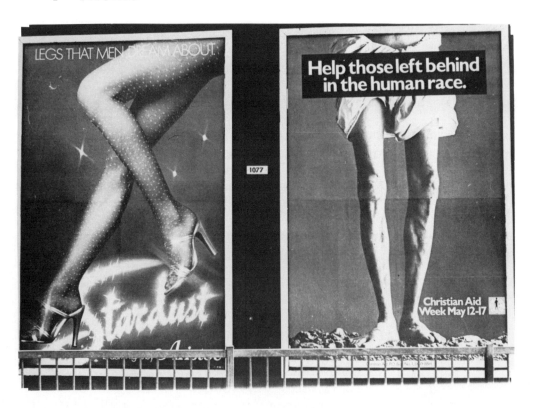

a) Which of the two posters would you be more inclined to notice?
b) Talk about the contrasts between them. What effect do they have on you?
c) Can you say that you are indifferent to either one or both of the posters? Is there a difference between your feelings now and your possible reactions, or lack of them, if you saw the posters side by side in the street?

2.1 Text A

As you listen to the poem, see if you can catch Emily Dickinson's attitude to the world's indifferences.

I'm Nobody! Who are you?
Are you – Nobody – Too?
Then there's a pair of us?
Don't tell! they'd advertise – you know!

How dreary – to be – Somebody!   5
How public – like a Frog –
To tell one's name – the livelong June –
To an admiring Bog!

Emily Dickinson, *Nobody*

a) Do you find the punctuation unusual? What is its effect?
b) Why does she say 'Don't tell'? What gesture often accompanies this expression?
c) Who are 'they' (l.4)? Why do you think 'they'd advertise'?
d) What makes a frog 'public' in the month of June?

2.2 Spend a few minutes thinking about the following, then discuss them with a partner.
a) Do you consider yourself a 'Nobody' or a 'Somebody'?
b) What are the advantages and disadvantages of being a 'Nobody', and those of being a 'Somebody'?
c) Are there things in which you *want* to be noticed by the world, and others which you do not care about?

3.1 Text B

John Clare's feelings are quite the opposite of Emily Dickinson's. As you read the poem, pick out the words and phrases which you think best express the poet's feelings of loss and regret. What would he prefer to have instead of suffering the indifference of mankind?

⟫⟶

61

Indifference

I am: yet what I am none cares or knows,
  My friends forsake me like a memory lost;
I am the self-consumer of my woes,
  They rise and vanish in oblivious host,
Like shades in love and death's oblivion lost;   5
And yet I am, and live with shadows tost

Into the nothingness of scorn and noise,
  Into the living sea of waking dreams,
Where there is neither sense of life nor joys,
  But the vast shipwreck of my life's esteems;   10
And een the dearest—that I loved the best—
Are strange—nay, rather stranger than the rest.

I long for scenes where man has never trod;
  A place where woman never smiled or wept;
There to abide with my Creator, God,   15
  And sleep as I in childhood sweetly slept;
Untroubling and untroubled where I lie;
The grass below—above the vaulted sky.

John Clare, *I am*

a) What do you find positive in the poem?
b) Do the positive aspects compensate for the negative ones?
c) What things *were* important to the poet, as expressed in the first
   two verses? Why have they lost their importance to him?
d) Why does he want to return to his childhood? Is this just an idealistic
   dream, or do you think he can recover some of his lost innocence?
e) What do you think lines 7 and 8 are talking about?
f) Why might your dearest friends seem 'stranger than the rest' (l.12)?
g) What do you think Clare means by 'esteems' (l.10)? Are they more
   or less than ideals or ambitions?
h) Can you identify with Clare's vision, or is it too personal for that?

3.2 The metaphor of 'the living sea' in line 8 expresses the chaos of life and
relates to another metaphor in a later line.
a) Find the second, related metaphor.
b) Discuss the relationship between the two metaphors.
c) There are similes as well as metaphors in the poem. Find them.
d) What does the poem gain from figurative expression (simile and
   metaphor in this case)?

3.3 Have you noticed the great number of 's' sounds in the poem? Try reading it aloud. Do they achieve any special effect?

4.1 Text C

Christopher Isherwood, in Berlin in the 1930s, observes various reactions to the growing threat of war, on an evening when Hitler is due to make a speech which will be broadcast on the radio. As you read you will find several different reactions to the crisis. The first reaction is described as 'insensitive'; make notes of adjectives describing other reactions, including Isherwood's own.

To make the time pass, I got my hair cut. At the barber's, a hateful jaundiced-looking customer was talking confidently about the certainty of war; trying to make the manicure girl's flesh creep. He didn't succeed. She was another of the insensitive ones. But another customer agreed with relish, "Why read the papers? They'll tell us soon enough when it comes. Then we'll be under orders." (This last remark struck a clear note of satisfaction. *Orders*—that's what they deeply want.)

Then I went into a cinema. Nearly always this kills my time-and-place sense; yesterday it wasn't even dulled. I felt absolutely toxic with crisis. The newsreel contained no scenes whatsoever of Hitler or the Nazis. Was this deliberate policy? Anyhow, it seemed fatally ostrich-like. I prefer to be reminded of them, every instant. The film itself bored me, except for a few moments when you were shown somebody being happy—a little girl laughing for no reason, a fat man enjoying his beer. This was almost unbearable, because their happiness seemed so poignantly insecure. My eyes filled with tears. Once I found myself actually beginning to sob. I turned it into a cough.

And then an old man just behind me started muttering to himself. He was either drunk or half out of his mind. "Oh, I do want to die! Oh, I'm so ill! My wife hates me. She says: Why don't you poison yourself? Go on out to the cinema. I'm sick of you. . . . Oh, I do want to die—" The old man kept repeating this, until I couldn't stand it and had to leave. No one else seemed to hear him.

I had to have supper with Aunt Edith, so there was no question of being able to listen to the speech itself. (Even if Aunt E. had stooped to the vulgarity of owning a wireless set, she'd probably still have refused to listen. She'd feel that it was somehow encouraging and abetting "that odious man," as she

63

calls him.) So we talked family gossip, and I kept glancing in misery at the grandfather clock and thinking, "Now he's begun . . . now he's got to the middle . . . by this time he must have said the word—*if* he's going to say it." 35

I excused myself as early as I could, and rushed over to Dr Fisch in a taxi. He says the speech has altered nothing. It was very violent but carefully vague. "You see, Christopher, violence is never alarming—what is alarming is lack of violence. The situation now becomes perfectly clear. The neutrality of 40 Czechoslovakia will be guaranteed on condition her French and Russian alliances are dropped. Oh, yes, naturally, the crisis will continue. And one must never discount the possibility of incidents. But that is really irrelevant. One has to learn to analyze these things from an objective, dialectical viewpoint; 45 and not—excuse me that I say this—with the emotionalism of the popular press." This last was a playful little dig at me, of course, because I had admitted to him how worried I've been. But I didn't care; I was much too relieved.

Christopher Isherwood, *Down There on a Visit*

a) Christopher visits four places. Describe how he makes the presence of the crisis felt in all four.
b) Explain the following phrases in your own words:
   – trying to make the manicure girl's *flesh creep* (l.4)
   – my *time-and-place sense* (ll.9-10)
   – *ostrich-like* (l.13)
   – *so poignantly insecure* (ll.17-18)
   – *encouraging and abetting* (l.31)
   – a *playful little dig* at me (l.47)
c) Who is 'that odious man' (l.31)? Who is 'he' (ll.34–35)?
d) Who do you feel most sympathy with and/or most sorry for?

4.2 Discuss in groups of three or four.
a) Dr Fisch says, 'violence is never alarming – what is alarming is lack of violence'. (ll.38-39) What do you think he means by this?
b) Is indifference, or lack of response, more worrying than a strong reaction to a situation?
c) Think of a situation in your own experience which in your view required a strong response. What was *your* reaction, and what were the reactions of others?
d) Can indifference ever be considered in a positive light?

5.1 Text D

W.H. Auden uses a painting by Breughel to show how 'life goes on', indifferent to a crisis or one person's tragedy – in this case the death of Icarus, the boy who, trying to fly, went too near the sun so that the wax holding his wings together melted and he fell into the sea.

About suffering they were never wrong,
The Old Masters: how well they understood
Its human position; how it takes place
While someone else is eating or opening a window or just walking
    dully along;   5
How, when the aged are reverently, passionately waiting
For the miraculous birth, there always must be
Children who did not specially want it to happen, skating
On a pond at the edge of the wood:
They never forgot   10
That even the dreadful martyrdom must run its course
Anyhow in a corner, some untidy spot
Where the dogs go on with their doggy life and the torturer's horse
Scratches its innocent behind on a tree.
          ⟫→

In Breughel's *Icarus,* for instance: how everything turns away   15
Quite leisurely from the disaster; the ploughman may
Have heard the splash, the forsaken cry,
But for him it was not an important failure; the sun shone
As it had to on the white legs disappearing into the green
Water; and the expensive delicate ship that must have seen   20
Something amazing, a boy falling out of the sky,
Had somewhere to get to and sailed calmly on.

W.H. Auden, *Musée des Beaux Arts*

a) Who are 'they' (ll.1,2,10)? What did they understand, and never
    forget?
b) There are many words and phrases which express the normality of
    ordinary life – all of line 4, for example. What other words or
    phrases or lines emphasise normality?
c) What do you think the 'miraculous birth' (l.7) might be?
d) What things mentioned in the poem can you find in the painting
    Auden describes?
e) Why do you think 'everything turns away / Quite leisurely from the
    disaster'?
f) What would you have done?

5.2   In Auden's poem there are many contrasts between strong words like
'reverently' and casual words like 'dully'. List such contrasting words,
then discuss the special effects they achieve.

6.1 Text E 📼

Dylan Thomas explains why he finds it essential to remain indifferent
in some circumstances.

Never until the mankind making
Bird beast and flower
Fathering and all humbling darkness
Tells with silence the last light breaking
And the still hour   5
Is come of the sea tumbling in harness

And I must enter again the round
Zion of the water bead
And the synagogue of the ear of corn
Shall I let pray the shadow of a sound   10
Or sow my salt seed
In the least valley of sackcloth to mourn

The majesty and burning of the child's death.
I shall not murder
The mankind of her going with a grave truth   15
Nor blaspheme down the stations of the breath
With any further
Elegy of innocence and youth.

Deep with the first dead lies London's daughter,
Robed in the long friends,   20
The grains beyond age, the dark veins of her mother,
Secret by the unmourning water
Of the riding Thames.
After the first death, there is no other.

Dylan Thomas, *A Refusal to Mourn the Death, by Fire, of a Child in London*

a) Work out the sentence structure of the first 13 lines by thinking about the relationships between 'Never', 'until', 'Shall I'.
b) What is the subject of 'Tells' (l.4)? What does it tell?
c) Most of the other words in lines 1 to 3 are adjectives qualifying 'darkness'. Can you identify and explain three composite adjectives in these lines?
d) What will happen to the sea?
e) Where will the poet ('I') 'enter again' (l.7)?
f) What does 'sow my salt seed' mean in the context of mourning?
g) The third verse exalts the girl's death, and makes anything the poet might say worthless. What words show the negative effect his words would have?
h) What double meanings are there in 'a grave truth' (l.15) and 'stations' (l.16)?
i) Who do you think 'the first dead' (l.19) are, and whose 'the first death' (l.24) is?
j) Who or what are 'the long friends' (l.20)?

k) Apart from the poet, who or what does not mourn?
l) The third verse seems to imply that the poet is *not* indifferent to the child's death. Do you agree?
m) When will the poet mourn? Why not till then?

6.2 Are we *necessarily* indifferent to some of the suffering in the world? Why? Discuss this point in relation to Dylan Thomas's poem and then write a piece about a time when you were indifferent to circumstances that were tragic for others. To what do you attribute your indifference?

7 Simulation

The town has grown, standards of living have improved, and the inhabitants are content with their daily routine. But there is a general condition of indifference. When the last remaining green area in the town was converted into a mammoth shopping centre, there was no public reaction at all. When there was news of a possible world war, the events as reported by the mass media seemed distant and irrelevant. Other events have taken place in recent years to which one would expect strong reactions, but to which there has been no public response. You, the class, are trying to tackle this problem of public indifference.

a) Meet in small groups (4 or 5). What situations would you expect the inhabitants of the town to care about passionately? For example:
   – The increased use of corporal punishment in schools;
   – The closing of the one remaining theatre;
   – The need for pedestrian precincts.
   Include these in your list if you wish.
b) Tell the other groups about the situations you have listed. Make a composite list of about eight situations.
c) Working individually, make some notes on action that could be taken to shake the townspeople's indifference with respect to the situations you have collectively decided upon.
d) You have decided to bombard the local press with letters about the situations you have discussed. Select one of them and write your letter. If you wish, you can write as if you are one of the following:
   a local clergyman
   a social worker
   the headmaster of a school
   a town councillor
   a youth club leader

8 The language of indifference and the language of caring

a) Examine the texts in this unit and try to distinguish between language which expresses or describes an *indifferent* attitude, and the language of a *caring* attitude. In the Isherwood passage, for example, 'I felt absolutely toxic with crisis' is *caring*, while 'The film itself bored me' is *indifferent*.

b) Think of an event, a film you have seen, or a book you have read, which in your view would affect most people emotionally. Write about it with indifference in a diary of your daily life.

POSTSCRIPT

The worst sin towards our fellow creatures is not to hate them, but to be indifferent to them; that's the essence of inhumanity.

G.B. Shaw, *The Devil's Disciple*

7 Rebellion

The be-all and end-all

1.1 Theme

a) Tell your teacher what you think is happening in the photograph.
b) Look more carefully at the details and discuss how these contribute to the general impression of violence.
c) Have *you* ever witnessed a similar scene? Tell the class about it. How did it begin and develop, and what were the results?
d) Does any good ever come of violence?

1.2 Use your dictionary to investigate similarities and differences between the meanings of the following. (Some of them will appear in the next passage.) Then tell your partner what you have found out.

rebel	uprising
rebellion	clash
revolt	protest
revolution	demonstration

2.1 Text A 📼

When you have read the text, write down your answers to the questions in note form. Then, working with a partner, tell each other as much as you can about the Rebellion.

Now, as it turned out, the Rebellion was achieved much earlier and more easily than anyone had expected. In past years Mr Jones, although a hard master, had been a capable farmer, but of late he had fallen on evil days. He had become much 5 disheartened after losing money in a lawsuit, and had taken to drinking more than was good for him. For whole days at a time he would lounge in his Windsor chair in the kitchen, reading the newspapers, drinking, and occasionally feeding Moses 10 on crusts of bread soaked in beer. His men were idle and dishonest, the fields were full of weeds, the buildings wanted roofing, the hedges were neglected, and the animals were underfed.

June came and the hay was almost ready for 15 cutting. On Midsummer's Eve, which was a Saturday, Mr Jones went into Willingdon and got so drunk at the Red Lion that he did not come back till midday on Sunday. The men had milked the cows in the early morning and then had gone out 20 rabbiting, without bothering to feed the animals. When Mr Jones got back he immediately went to sleep on the drawing-room sofa with the *News of the World* over his face, so that when evening came, the animals were still unfed. At last they could stand it 25 no longer. One of the cows broke in the door of the store-shed with her horns and all the animals began to help themselves from the bins. It was just then that Mr Jones woke up. The next moment he and his four men were in the store-shed with whips in 30 their hands, lashing out in all directions. This was more than the hungry animals could bear. With one accord, though nothing of the kind had been planned beforehand, they flung themselves upon their tormentors. Jones and his men suddenly found 35

⟫→

71

themselves being butted and kicked from all sides.
The situation was quite out of their control. They
had never seen animals behave like this before, and
this sudden uprising of creatures whom they were
used to thrashing and maltreating just as they chose,   40
frightened them almost out of their wits. After only
a moment or two they gave up trying to defend
themselves and took to their heels. A minute later
all five of them were in full flight down the cart-
track that led to the main road, with the animals   45
pursuing them in triumph.

George Orwell, *Animal Farm*

a) Why did the animals revolt?
b) What had been the change in Mr Jones in recent years, and what
   influence did it have on the men who worked for him?
c) Who, or what, do you think Moses is?
d) The animals had not planned a complete rebellion. Which sentences
   tell us this? Which sentence begins the first phase of the move
   towards the Rebellion? And what makes the animals react so
   strongly that they drive the humans away?
e) How long does the Rebellion take?
f) When does the Rebellion happen? When had the animals last been
   fed, as far as you can tell?
g) Do you think the animals' reaction was justified?

2.2   What did the animals do next? Discuss this first, then write a paragraph
or two describing what *you* think they did.

2.3   Do the following now, and then refer to your answers when you have
read Text B.
a) Pick out all the words of violence in the passage from *Animal Farm*.
b) Decide on possible reasons for Orwell's making his rebels animals.
   Why not human beings?
c) Decide whether the passage seems modern or old, and when it might
   have been written.

3.1   Text B   📼

John Milton, too, describes a rebellion. You almost certainly found
that you could read the Orwell passage relatively easily; you will not
find Milton easy. The instructions, questions and explanations are
designed to enable you to come to grips with the lines; they signpost
you to the clues, and make you aware of elements which are often, not
only in this text, obstacles to understanding.

a) i)   *Do not read the passage.* Begin by *listening to lines 32 to 44,*
either from the cassette or as read by your teacher. Listen to the
sounds and rhythms without worrying too much about the sense.
Then discuss what it is that Milton seems to be describing. Can
you remember any specific sounds and words which contribute
to the impression you have gained?

ii) Now read *only the lines that you have listened to (32–44)*. Does
your reading confirm your first impression? Discuss with a
partner, and pick out the words which are a key to the event that
is taking place.

> "God and nature bid the same,
> When he who rules is worthiest, and excels
> Them whom he governs. This is servitude,
> To serve the unwise, or him who hath rebelled
> Against his worthier, as thine now serve thee,   5
> Thy self not free, but to thy self enthralled;
> Yet lewdly dar'st our ministering upbraid.
> Reign thou in hell thy kingdom, let me serve
> In heaven God ever blest, and his divine
> Behests obey, worthiest to be obeyed,   10
> Yet chains in hell, not realms expect: mean while
> From me returned, as erst thou saidst, from flight,
> This greeting on thy impious crest receive."
>   So saying, a noble stroke he lifted high,
> Which hung not, but so swift with tempest fell   15
> On the proud crest of Satan, that no sight,
> Nor motion of swift thought, less could his shield
> Such ruin intercept: ten paces huge
> He back recoiled; the tenth on bended knee
> His massy spear upstayed; as if on earth   20
> Winds under ground or waters forcing way
> Sidelong, had pushed a mountain from his seat
> Half sunk with all his pines. Amazement seized
> The rebel thrones, but greater rage to see
> Thus foiled their mightiest, ours joy filled, and shout,   25
> Presage of victory and fierce desire
> Of battle: whereat Michaël bid sound   ⫸→

The archangel trumpet; through the vast of heaven
It sounded, and the faithful armies rung
Hosanna to the highest: nor stood at gaze   30
The adverse legions, nor less hideous joined
The horrid shock: now storming fury rose,
And clamour such as heard in heaven till now
Was never, arms on armour clashing brayed
Horrible discord, and the madding wheels   35
Of brazen chariots raged; dire was the noise
Of conflict; over head the dismal hiss
Of fiery darts in flaming volleys flew,
And flying vaulted either host with fire.
  So under fiery cope together rushed   40
Both battles main, with ruinous assault
And inextinguishable rage; all heaven
Resounded, and had earth been then, all earth
Had to her centre shook.

John Milton, *Paradise Lost*

b) i) The *cause* of the events you have read about is described in lines
       14–32. Read and listen to these lines simultaneously, and first
       try to work out what actions the following perform:
           he (l.14)
           Satan (l.16)
           The rebel thrones (l.24)
           Michaël (l.27)
           the faithful armies (l.29)
           The adverse legions (l.31)
   ii) Work with a partner.
       We cannot have much understanding of the passage without
       knowing:
       – who 'he' is (l.14).
         His name is not mentioned here, but what actions does he
         perform in the passage? What characteristics does he seem to
         have? Does he seem to have Milton's sympathy, or not?
       – who Satan is.
         This is easier!
       – who Michaël is.
         Not so easy, but if you were to choose from a list of famous
         Michaels, you would now find it easy to identify him.
       – who the groups are: 'The rebel thrones', 'the faithful armies',
         'The adverse legions'.
         You might be able to guess at this point, as this is knowledge
         which can be derived from Milton's text.

c) You might now have arrived at Milton's subject in *Paradise Lost*.
Satan and his followers were expelled by God from Heaven for
disobedience. This extract describes the battle between the powers
of Heaven and Hell.
The 'he' referred to in line 14 is Abdiel, the faithful angel who
withstood Satan when he urged the angels to revolt. Michaël was
the great prince of all the angels and leader of the celestial armies.
The events are narrated by Raphael, whom Milton described as the
'sociable spirit' and the 'affable archangel'.

d) Work with a partner.
  i) Now read lines 1–13 and decide who is speaking – one of God's
     or one of Satan's men? How can you tell?
  ii) The difficulty of the first 13 lines is largely due to the fact that,
     because we are looking at an *extract* and not the complete work,
     and we 'come to it cold', it is difficult to reconstruct the speaker's
     context. But there are other problems: the number of abstrac-
     tions, the complex sentence structure with superlatives and
     comparatives, the pronouns. Before going on to (iii) to (vi), look
     up in your dictionary any words in lines 1–13 that you are not
     sure of.
  iii) What do 'God and nature bid' (l.1)? Who is 'worthiest' and
     'worthier' (ll.2,5), and what does this worthiness contrast with
     in line 4?
  iv) What, according to the speaker, is 'servitude' (l.3)? Is he happy
     to serve (see ll.8–9)? Do you think he would agree that it is
     'better to reign in Hell than serve in Heaven'?
  v) Who are 'thine' and 'thee' (l.5)? 'He' (ll.2–3) is not the same as
     'him'/'his' (ll.4–5). Who do they refer to?
  vi) What, according to the speaker, can Satan and his followers
     expect in Hell? (See l.11.)

e) Many of the sentences have an unfamiliar word order, to heighten
   the poetic effect. You can rewrite the final two lines
           'and, had earth been then, all earth
   Had to her centre shook'.
   to read:
   'and all earth, if earth had existed then, would have shaken to her
   centre'.

   Rewrite the following lines in the same way:
       11 – 13 ('Yet...receive')
       18 – 19 ('ten paces...recoiled')
       32 – 34 ('now...never')
   Do you think that Milton's lines are more dramatically effective
   than your versions? If so, what is it that makes them more effective?

3.2 Discuss the following questions with your teacher. They are all concerned with the styles and effectiveness of the passages by Orwell and
Milton.
a) How do the authors convey the violence of the rebellions?
b) Why do you think Milton wrote in verse and Orwell in prose? Do
the authors' attitudes to rebellion and rebels have anything to do
with this, do you think?
c) Does Milton's poem remind you of any poetry in your own language? If so, when was it written?
d) Can you suggest when Milton's poem might have been written?
e) Do you think it is necessary, or desirable, to know the historical
background to texts like these? Why or why not?

4.1 Text C

Macbeth, in Shakespeare's play, is on the point of committing the
ultimate act of rebellion – he is going to kill King Duncan.
a) First *listen* to the soliloquy. What do its rhythms, and Macbeth's
pauses, suggest to you?
b) Then *read* it. As you read, note the positive and negative possibilities
Macbeth sees in the intended action. Also, prepare to answer the
following questions.
 – Will the action of killing Duncan be over quickly, or will it have
   consequences?
 – What reasons does Macbeth give for *not* killing Duncan?
 – What is the only reason he has for killing Duncan?

Macbeth.   If it were done, when 'tis done, then 'twere well
It were done quickly: if th'assassination
Could trammel up the consequence, and catch,
With his surcease, success; that but this blow
Might be the be-all and the end-all . . . here,   5
But here, upon this bank and shoal of time,
We'ld jump the life to come. But in these cases
We still have judgement here—that we but teach
Bloody instructions, which being taught return
To plague th'inventor: this even-handed justice   10
Commends th'ingredience of our poisoned chalice
To our own lips. He's here in double trust:
First, as I am his kinsman and his subject,
Strong both against the deed; then, as his host,
Who should against his murderer shut the door,   15
Not bear the knife myself. Besides, this Duncan

Hath borne his faculties so meek, hath been
So clear in his great office, that his virtues
Will plead like angels, trumpet-tongued, against
The deep damnation of his taking-off: 20
And pity, like a naked new-born babe,
Striding the blast, or Heaven's cherubin, horsed
Upon the sightless couriers of the air,
Shall blow the horrid deed in every eye,
That tears shall drown the wind. I have no spur   25
To prick the sides of my intent, but only
Vaulting ambition, which o'erleaps itself,
And falls on th'other—

William Shakespeare, *Macbeth*

4.2 a) What is 'it' in the first two lines?
b) Use your dictionary to check the vocabulary, then rewrite in your
own words the first seven lines ('If...life to come').
c) You might have noticed that there are some words which do not
help the meaning, and that some of the thought is confused. How
might this reflect Macbeth's state of mind? Does it relate in any way
to the rhythms and pauses that you listened for?
d) What is the threat to Macbeth in lines 8–12?
e) What do we learn about the character of Duncan? Why does
Shakespeare make the contrast between 'angels' and 'damnation'
(ll. 19–20)? Is this similar to the conflict we saw in *Paradise Lost*?
f) How many images of horses and riding can you find in lines 22–28?
What impression of danger do they give you?
g) Do you think Macbeth intends to say another word after 'th'other'
(l.28)? If so, what might it be? Does he think he might fall?
h) By the end of the soliloquy, do you think Macbeth is ready to kill
Duncan, or is he still uncertain?

5.1 Text D 🔈

In our own time, many movements, groups and parties have been
involved in similar problems of rebellion. Terrorism – short, sharp, and
very violent – is a common means to this end.
As you read the passage by Iris Murdoch, make notes which enable you
to answer the following questions, and then discuss your answers in
groups of four or five.

⟫→

Rebellion

a) Why do you think the two young men shoot the people in the airport lounge?
b) What weapons do they use?
c) Have you heard or read of any similar acts recently?
d) Do you think rebellion in this form is justifiable?

'Policemen!' said Luca.

Harriet looked up. There was a curious group of uniformed men standing in the doorway of the lounge. Harriet stared. The tense still attitudes of the men announced something unusual. Danger. Harriet's 5 heart suddenly began to beat very fast. She turned and saw next to her a stout German whom she had noticed on the plane. His face struck her with terror. It had gone completely white, his mouth open, his eyes staring towards the centre of the room. Harriet 10 looked there. In the midst of a deadly quietness and frozen immobility of everybody else, two young men were standing together, one of them holding a long glittering tube in his hands. More police appeared in another doorway. Someone called out peremptorily 15 in German. A woman screamed. One of the police- men raised a revolver. There was a sudden crackling of deafening sound and the room became full of desperate agonized screaming. The stout man beside Harriet fell to the floor bleeding profusely. Screaming 20 herself, Harriet covered Luca with her body.

Iris Murdoch, *The Sacred and Profane Love Machine*

5.2 The four texts in this unit deal with their inter-related themes in differing styles, to achieve different effects.
Work with a partner.
a) Choose from each of the texts one or two sentences which you find best characterise their style.
b) Try to say why you have chosen the sentences, and how they contrast with each other.

6 Simulation

a) You and a group of friends have strong feelings about ways in which terrorism should or should not be punished. You have just read about the situation described by Iris Murdoch in the newspaper. A discussion begins. In preparation for the discussion:
   – Write some notes on your own opinions.
   – Re-read the texts in this unit. What ideas do they give you that will be useful in the discussion?

b) The discussion. Come to a general agreement on appropriate treatment of terrorists. If there are major differences of opinion, take a vote.

c) Write a summary of the points that were raised in the discussion and the decisions taken, and add a paragraph expressing your own attitude.

7 Violent language

a) Make an examination of 'the language of violence' and 'violent language' in the texts. In sensational writing, this kind of language is exploited to the full, whereas in the texts in this unit it is used sparingly, and not just to startle the reader. Discuss this.

b) Write two passages:
   – A report of a violent incident that might appear in a popular newspaper.
   – An account of an incident in your own life which, from your point of view at least, was frightening in its violence.

POSTSCRIPT

Man was born free, and everywhere he is in chains.

Jean-Jacques Rousseau, *The Social Contract*

8 Ideals

'Tis not too late to seek a newer world.

1.1 Theme

VTOPIAE INSVLAE FIGVRA

Dante's ideals were embodied in Beatrice, a girl whom he adored from a distance and who guided him through Paradise in his *Divine Comedy*. Sir Thomas More's ideology found its expression in *Utopia*, an imaginary country.

a) Can you think of any other well-known embodiments of ideals?
b) Do you have ideals which find expression in some place or person, real or imaginary?

1.2 From Bertrand Russell's description of his 'governing passions', would you call him an idealist?

Three passions, simple but overwhelmingly strong, have governed my life: the longing for love, the search for knowledge, and unbearable pity for the suffering of mankind. These passions, like great winds, have blown me hither and thither, in a wayward course, over a deep ocean of anguish, reaching to the very verge of despair.   5

I have sought love, first, because it brings ecstasy – ecstasy so great that I would often have sacrificed all the rest of life for a few hours of this joy. I have sought it, next, because it relieves loneliness – that terrible loneliness in which one shivering consciousness looks over the rim of the world into the cold unfathomable lifeless abyss. I have sought it, finally,   10 because in the union of love I have seen, in a mystic miniature, the prefiguring vision of the heaven that saints and poets have imagined. This is what I sought, and though it might seem too good for human life, this is what – at least – I have found.

With equal passion I have sought knowledge. I have wished to under-   15 stand the hearts of men. I have wished to know why the stars shine. And I have tried to apprehend the Pythagorean power by which number holds sway over the flux. A little of this, but not much, I have achieved.

Love and knowledge, so far as they were possible, led upward toward the heavens. But always pity brought me back to earth. Echoes of cries of   20 pain reverberate in my heart. Children in famine, victims tortured by oppressors, helpless old people a hated burden to their sons, and the whole world of loneliness, poverty, and pain make a mockery of what human life should be. I long to alleviate the evil, but I cannot, and I too suffer.   25

This has been my life. I have found it worth living, and would gladly live it again if the chance were offered me.

Bertrand Russell, *Autobiography*

a) What does he mean by the 'upward' ideal (l.19)? What does it contrast with?
b) Do you agree that life as Russell describes it is worth living? What makes *your* life most worth living?

2.1 Text A 🖾

The passages we shall go on to read show various expressions of
Russell's contrast between the 'upward' ideal and the earthly contrast.
Rupert Brooke imagines what a fish might consider to be an ideal life.

Fish (fly-replete, in depth of June,
Dawdling away their wat'ry noon)
Ponder deep wisdom, dark or clear,
Each secret fishy hope or fear.
Fish say, they have their Stream and Pond;   5
But is there anything Beyond?
This life cannot be All, they swear,
For how unpleasant, if it were!
One may not doubt that, somehow, Good
Shall come of Water and of Mud;   10
And, sure, the reverent eye must see
A Purpose in Liquidity.
We darkly know, by Faith we cry,
The future is not Wholly Dry.
Mud unto mud!—Death eddies near—   15
Not here the appointed End, not here!
But somewhere, beyond Space and Time,
Is wetter water, slimier slime!
And there (they trust) there swimmeth One
Who swam ere rivers were begun,   20
Immense, of fishy form and mind,
Squamous, omnipotent, and kind;
And under that Almighty Fin,
The littlest fish may enter in.
Oh! never fly conceals a hook,   25
Fish say, in the Eternal Brook,
But more than mundane weeds are there,
And mud, celestially fair;
Fat caterpillars drift around,
And Paradisal grubs are found;   30
Unfading moths, immortal flies,
And the worm that never dies.
And in that Heaven of all their wish,
There shall be no more land, say fish.

Rupert Brooke, *Heaven*

Work with a partner.
a) Are the fishy 'hope or fear' and thoughts and dreams similar to human dreams and ideals? Pick out some lines which you think show such a similarity and say how you think they reflect human aspirations.
b) What are the fish doing at the beginning of the poem? Are they basically happy?
c) Are the fish optimistic?
d) Find the religious echoes in the poem. Many of them relate to the fishy God. Describe their God.
e) Often ideal worlds are simply better versions of the known world. List what fish would want *more* and *less* of in their Heaven.

2.2 Now think what *you* would want more or less of in your idea of Heaven. We said that 'ideal worlds are simply better versions of the known world'. What better versions of the known world can you think of?
Work in four groups.
a) Prepare an ideal world based on the workings of this world.
b) Compare your worlds.
c) Which world would be the best one to live in? And which is the easiest to believe in?

3.1 Text B

Listen to Coleridge's *Kubla Khan*. Which words give you the impression of a *lost* ideal?

In Xanadu did Kubla Khan
A stately pleasure-dome decree:
Where Alph, the sacred river, ran
Through caverns measureless to man
   Down to a sunless sea.   5
So twice five miles of fertile ground
With walls and towers were girdled round:
And there were gardens bright with sinuous rills,
Where blossomed many an incense-bearing tree;
And here were forests ancient as the hills,   10
Enfolding sunny spots of greenery.

But oh! that deep romantic chasm which slanted
Down the green hill athwart a cedarn cover!
A savage place! as holy and enchanted
As e'er beneath a waning moon was haunted   15   »»→

By woman wailing for her demon-lover!
And from this chasm, with ceaseless turmoil seething,
As if this earth in fast thick pants were breathing,
A mighty fountain momently was forced:
Amid whose swift half-intermitted burst   20
Huge fragments vaulted like rebounding hail,
Or chaffy grain beneath the thresher's flail:
And 'mid these dancing rocks at once and ever
It flung up momently the sacred river.
Five miles meandering with a mazy motion   25
Through wood and dale the sacred river ran,
Then reached the caverns measureless to man,
And sank in tumult to a lifeless ocean:
And 'mid this tumult Kubla heard from far
Ancestral voices prophesying war!   30
   The shadow of the dome of pleasure
   Floated midway on the waves;
   Where was heard the mingled measure
   From the fountain and the caves.
It was a miracle of rare device,   35
A sunny pleasure-dome with caves of ice!
   A damsel with a dulcimer
   In a vision once I saw:
   It was an Abyssinian maid,
   And on her dulcimer she played,   40
   Singing of Mount Abora.
   Could I revive within me
   Her symphony and song,
   To such a deep delight 'twould win me,
That with music loud and long,   45
I would build that dome in air,
That sunny dome! those caves of ice!
And all who heard should see them there,
And all should cry, Beware! Beware!
His flashing eyes, his floating hair!   50
Weave a circle round him thrice,
And close your eyes with holy dread,
For he on honey-dew hath fed,
And drunk the milk of Paradise.

Samuel Taylor Coleridge, *Kubla Khan*

a) The first two parts of the poem (ll.1–36) are description:
   i)   Of what?
   ii)   How big is it?
   iii) What grows there?
   iv) What two things emerge from the fountain?

       v)   What lines echo lines 3 to 5?

       vi)   What negative sound does Kubla hear?

       vii)   Who do you think Kubla Khan is?

       viii) What is the importance of 'decree' (l.2)? Do you think the 'pleasure-dome' was ever built, or only 'decreed'?

  b) The third part of the poem (ll.37–54) seems at first to have nothing to do with the earlier parts.

       i)   Who is speaking?

       ii)   What does he remember?

       iii)   What does he want to do with the vision? Why?

       iv)   What would be the result?

       v)   In what way would 'I' (l.46) or 'him' (l.51) be similar to Kubla Khan?

       vi)   Why should 'all...cry Beware! Beware!' (l.49)?

       vii)   What does the vision of the 'damsel with a dulcimer' (l.37) represent to the poet?

3.2 a) Here is a map which attempts to interpret the 'geography' of the poem. Do you agree with all of it? Examine it carefully in relation to the poem, change and add anything you wish, and then compare your version with those of others in the class.

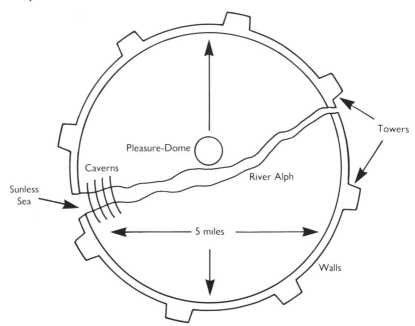

  b) Is it *possible* to draw the poem's geography? Does the attempt to do so throw any light on the meaning?

3.3 a) What is the relationship between the first two parts of the poem and the third part? Are the pleasure-dome and the vision of the damsel similar?

b) Most of the poem is written in the past tense. Pick out the lines which are in another tense. Can you say why they are not in the past tense? Why are the last two lines in the past tense?

c) Contrast the positive aspects of the vision with any negative aspects you have found. Is the poem a positive celebration of the vision, or does it express more regret at its transitory nature?

4.1 Text C 📼

Ideals can sometimes be misguided. Charles Dickens gives us a humorous, but concerned, picture of such a situation – exactly the opposite of 'Charity begins at home'. The chapter is entitled 'Telescopic Philanthropy'. As you read the passage, try to decide why the title is apposite, and note as many examples as you can of the neglect at home caused by Mrs Jellyby's devotion to 'the natives of Borrioboola-Gha'.

Nobody had appeared belonging to the house, except a person in pattens, who had been poking at the child from below with a broom; I don't know with what object, and I don't think she did. I therefore supposed that Mrs Jellyby was not at home; and was quite surprised when the person appeared in the passage without the pattens, and 5 going up to the back room on the first floor, before Ada and me, announced us as, 'Them two young ladies, Missis Jellyby!' We passed several more children on the way up, whom it was difficult to avoid treading on in the dark; and as we came into Mrs Jellyby's presence, one of the poor little things fell downstairs – down a whole 10 flight (as it sounded to me), with a great noise.

Mrs Jellyby, whose face reflected none of the uneasiness which we could not help showing in our own faces, as the dear child's head recorded its passage with a bump on every stair – Richard afterwards said he counted seven, besides one for the landing – received us with 15 perfect equanimity. She was a pretty, very diminutive, plump woman, of from forty to fifty, with handsome eyes, though they had a curious habit of seeming to look a long way off. As if – I am quoting Richard again – they could see nothing nearer than Africa!

'I am very glad indeed,' said Mrs Jellyby in an agreeable voice, 'to 20 have the pleasure of receiving you. I have a great respect for Mr Jarndyce; and no one in whom he is interested can be an object of indifference to me.'

We expressed our acknowledgements, and sat down behind the door where there was a lame invalid of a sofa. Mrs Jellyby had very 25

good hair, but was too much occupied with her African duties to
brush it. The shawl in which she had been loosely muffled, dropped
onto her chair when she advanced to us; and as she turned to resume
her seat, we could not help noticing that her dress didn't nearly
meet up the back, and that the open space was railed across with a   30
lattice-work of stay-lace – like a summer-house.

    The room, which was strewn with papers and nearly filled by a
great writing-table covered with similar litter, was, I must say, not
only very untidy, but very dirty. We were obliged to take notice of
that with our sense of sight, even while, with our sense of hearing,   35
we followed the poor child who had tumbled downstairs: I think into
the back kitchen, where somebody seemed to stifle him.

    But what principally struck us was a jaded and unhealthy-looking,
though by no means plain girl, at the writing-table, who sat biting
the feather of her pen, and staring at us. I suppose nobody ever was   40
in such a state of ink. And, from her tumbled hair to her pretty feet,
which were disfigured with frayed and broken satin slippers trodden
down at heel, she really seemed to have no article of dress upon her,
from a pin upwards, that was in its proper condition or its right
place.   45

    'You find me, my dears,' said Mrs Jellyby, snuffing the two great
office candles in tin candlesticks which made the room taste strongly
of hot tallow (the fire had gone out and there was nothing in the
grate but ashes, a bundle of wood, and a poker), 'you find me, my
dears, as usual, very busy; but that you will excuse. The African   50
project at present employs my whole time. It involves me in
correspondence with public bodies, and with private individuals
anxious for the welfare of their species all over the country. I am
happy to say it is advancing. We hope by this time next year to have
from a hundred and fifty to two hundred healthy families cultivating   55
coffee and educating the natives of Borrioboola-Gha, on the left
bank of the Niger.'

    As Ada said nothing, but looked at me, I said it must be very
gratifying.

    'It *is* gratifying,' said Mrs Jellyby. 'It involves the devotion of all   60
my energies, such as they are; but that is nothing, so that it
succeeds; and I am more confident of success every day. Do you
know, Miss Summerson, I almost wonder that *you* never turned your
thoughts to Africa.'

    This application of the subject was really so unexpected to me,   65
that I was quite at a loss how to receive it. I hinted that the
climate—

    'The finest climate in the world!' said Mrs Jellyby.

    'Indeed, ma'am?'

    'Certainly. With precaution,' said Mrs Jellyby. 'You may go into   70
Holborn, without precaution, and be run over. You may go into

⟫→

87

Holborn, with precaution, and never be run over. Just so with
Africa.'

I said, 'No doubt.' – I meant as to Holborn.

'If you would like,' said Mrs Jellyby, putting a number of papers   75
towards us, 'to look over some remarks on that head, and on the
general subject (which have been extensively circulated), while I
finish a letter I am now dictating to my eldest daughter, who is my
amanuensis—'

The girl at the table left off biting her pen, and made a return to   80
our recognition, which was half bashful and half sulky.

'—I shall then have finished for the present,' proceeded Mrs
Jellyby, with a sweet smile; 'though my work is never done. Where
are you, Caddy?'

'"Presents her compliments to Mr Swallow, and begs—"' said   85
Caddy.

'"And begs,"' said Mrs Jellyby, dictating, '"to inform him, in
reference to his letter of inquiry on the African project—" No,
Peepy! Not on any account!'

Peepy (so self-named) was the unfortunate child who had fallen   90
downstairs, who now interrupted the correspondence by presenting
himself with a strip of plaster on his forehead, to exhibit his
wounded knees, in which Ada and I did not know which to pity
most – the bruises or the dirt. Mrs Jellyby merely added, with the
serene composure with which she said everything, 'Go along, you   95
naughty Peepy!' and fixed her fine eyes on Africa again.

Charles Dickens, *Bleak House*

a) Who is telling the story? Is the narrator alone?
b) How many of Mrs Jellyby's children are named?
c) Richard is not present during the scene, but there are some words
    which tell us what he thinks of the Jellyby household. What are
    they?
d) Dickens's humour often emerges from a simple choice of words –
    for example, 'a person' (l.1), 'poking' (l.2), 'recorded its passage'
    (l.14) – which are graphic but not serious enough to make us worry.
    Find some more words or phrases which humorously underline the
    unhappiness of the situation.
e) How many individual examples of Mrs Jellyby's neglect can you
    find?
f) Describe the narrator's attitude to the Jellybys.
g) What is Dickens criticising in this passage?
h) Discuss why 'Telescopic Philanthropy' is an apposite title for the
    chapter.

4.2 Class discussion.
Can you think of any other examples of blind idealism? Can you justify any of them? Is it true that 'Charity begins at home'?

5.1 Text D

Our final idealist is a world-famous hero, Ulysses, or Odysseus, the hero of Homer's *Odyssey*. What do you know about him? He is speaking of a time long after his triumphant return from Troy, when he is again restless. As you read, note down his reasons for wanting to 'drink Life to the lees' (ll.6–7). What does he mean by that?

It little profits that an idle king,
By this still hearth, among these barren crags,
Match'd with an aged wife, I mete and dole
Unequal laws unto a savage race,
That hoard, and sleep, and feed, and know not me.   5
I cannot rest from travel: I will drink
Life to the lees: all times I have enjoy'd
Greatly, have suffer'd greatly, both with those
That loved me, and alone; on shore, and when
Thro' scudding drifts the rainy Hyades   10
Vext the dim sea: I am become a name;
For always roaming with a hungry heart
Much have I seen and known; cities of men
And manners, climates, councils, governments,
Myself not least, but honour'd of them all;   15
And drunk delight of battle with my peers,
Far on the ringing plains of windy Troy.
I am a part of all that I have met;
Yet all experience is an arch wherethro'
Gleams that untravell'd world, whose margin fades   20
For ever and for ever when I move.
How dull it is to pause, to make an end,
To rust unburnish'd, not to shine in use!
As tho' to breathe were life. Life piled on life
Were all too little, and of one to me   25
Little remains: but every hour is saved
From that eternal silence, something more,
A bringer of new things; and vile it were
For some three suns to store and hoard myself,
And this gray spirit yearning in desire   30
To follow knowledge like a sinking star,
Beyond the utmost bound of human thought.

⟫→

   This is my son, mine own Telemachus,
To whom I leave the sceptre and the isle—
Well-loved of me, discerning to fulfil   35
This labour, by slow prudence to make mild
A rugged people, and thro' soft degrees
Subdue them to the useful and the good.
Most blameless is he, centred in the sphere
Of common duties, decent not to fail   40
In offices of tenderness, and pay
Meet adoration to my household gods,
When I am gone. He works his work, I mine.
   There lies the port; the vessel puffs her sail:
There gloom the dark broad seas. My mariners,   45
Souls that have toil'd, and wrought, and thought with me—
That ever with a frolic welcome took
The thunder and the sunshine, and opposed
Free hearts, free foreheads—you and I are old;
Old age hath yet his honour and his toil;   50
Death closes all: but something ere the end,
Some work of noble note, may yet be done,
Not unbecoming men that strove with Gods.
The lights begin to twinkle from the rocks:
The long day wanes: the slow moon climbs: the deep   55
Moans round with many voices. Come, my friends,
'Tis not too late to seek a newer world.
Push off, and sitting well in order smite
The sounding furrows; for my purpose holds
To sail beyond the sunset, and the baths   60
Of all the western stars, until I die.
It may be that the gulfs will wash us down:
It may be we shall touch the Happy Isles,
And see the great Achilles, whom we knew.
Tho' much is taken, much abides; and tho'   65
We are not now that strength which in old days
Moved earth and heaven; that which we are, we are;
One equal temper of heroic hearts,
Made weak by time and fate, but strong in will
To strive, to seek, to find, and not to yield.   70

Alfred, Lord Tennyson, *Ulysses*

a) Ulysses gives signs of dissatisfaction with the present (ll.1–5). What
   are they?
b) What are the contrasts in lines 7 to 11?
c) What words recall Ulysses's fame?

d) What is the 'untravell'd world' (l.20)?
e) In line 24, does he mean that 'to breathe' is 'life'?
f) To what does 'of one' (l.25) refer?
g) What is 'something more, A bringer of new things' (ll.27–28)? How can you tell it is not death?
h) What contrast is there between Telemachus and Ulysses?
i) Whose are the 'Free hearts, free foreheads' (l.49)?
j) What noun(s) does the adjective 'unbecoming' (l.53) qualify?
k) To whom does he give the order 'Push off' (l.58)? What must they then do, in your own words?
l) Do they have a specific destination when they leave?
m) Why do they go?
n) Do you think line 55 has a wider meaning than the simple description it gives?
o) Can you identify or sympathise with Ulysses?

5.2 Class discussion.
What similarities and contrasts do you notice between Ulysses and Bertrand Russell? How do their attitudes to life seem to relate to those of Coleridge and Mrs Jellyby?

6 Simulation

a) Think back to the ideal world that you envisaged in 2.2 (c), the one you selected as being the best to live in.
b) You are going to set off as a community to make your ideal world a reality. Make notes on how you see any of the following in your ideal world; show contrasts with the real world:
    architecture   education   entertainment
    the balance between work and leisure   the press   family life
    relationships between the generations   government   food
c) Find someone else in the community who has made notes on the same aspect as yourself. Discuss similarities and differences in your attitudes.
d) Prepare to talk about your attitude to the aspect you have chosen. Your talk will be delivered to the assembled Planning Committee, and will last a maximum of one and a half minutes.
e) The preliminary meeting of the Planning Committee. Each member has a maximum of one and a half minutes to describe his/her personal vision of one aspect of life in the ideal world you intend to make a reality.

⟫→

f) You wish to attract more members to work on the creation of your ideal world. Write *one* of the following:
   - A letter to *The Times* reporting on the Planning Committee's preliminary meeting.
   - An article for a magazine of your own choice, describing your ideal world.
   - A letter to a relative in another country, describing your personal attitudes to the ideal world and what you expect from it.

7 The language of ideals

The language that an author chooses when writing about ideals tends to be extreme or far-fetched. Notice the recurrence of 'search' and 'sought' in the Bertrand Russell passage. How does 'seek' differ from 'look for'? Brooke's poem has words like 'wisdom' and 'Faith'. Look through the passages in the unit and find the words and phrases which convey the abstract, other-worldly, or any other side of ideals.

POSTSCRIPT

After all has been said that can be said about the widening influence of ideas, it remains true that they would hardly be such strong agents unless they were taken in a solvent of feeling. The great world-struggle of developing thought is continually foreshadowed in the struggle of the affections, seeking a justification for love and hope.

George Eliot, *Romola*

9 Ambitions

What's a heaven for?

1.1 Theme

Many of us have small ambitions that we would never admit to: things we would like to make happen, but which never will happen. Have you ever, like this character, imagined your ambitions being realised?

—I'd like to be able to raise me hand in a crowded room with everyone rabbiting away like buggery, and there'd be silence. They'd keep on opening and 5 shutting their mouths, but no sound would come out. And they'd all panic. They'd scream, and not a sound would they make. They'd stamp their feet on the floor, they'd 10 hammer at the door, and there'd be no sound. They'd start smashing things—glasses, cups, dinner plates, egg cups—and all would be silence. And then I'd 15 raise me hand again, and I'd start to laugh. And that would be real. They'd hear that. Just my laughter and nowt else. And then the birds would start to sing, and they'd 20 hear them. And then a weasel would sink its teeth into a rabbit's spine, and it'd scream. They'd hear that right enough. By God, they would. 25

Peter Tinniswood, *I Didn't Know You Cared*

Other ambitions are on a grander scale.

Nature that framed us of four
  elements,
Warring within our breasts for
  regiment,
Doth teach us all to have
  aspiring minds:
Our souls whose faculties can
  comprehend
The wondrous architecture of
  the world: 5
And measure every wandering
  planet's course,
Still climbing after knowledge
  infinite,
And always moving as the
  restless spheres,
Wills us to wear ourselves and
  never rest,
Until we reach the ripest fruit of 10
  all,
That perfect bliss and sole
  felicity,
The sweet fruition of an earthly
  crown.

Christopher Marlowe, *Tamburlaine*

a) Do you have an 'aspiring
   mind'?
b) What ambitions do you have?
c) What do you think is meant
   by 'an *earthly* crown'?

1.2   a) Spend a few minutes thinking about yourself and your past and
present ambitions. Make some notes on ambitions you feel you have
already achieved, and those which you are still working towards.

b) In groups of three or four, share your experiences of ambitions,
achieved and current. You may, of course, have an ambition you
prefer not to admit to; decide for yourself *why* you want to keep it
to yourself. Comment on each other's experiences in any way you
wish.

1.3   Remain in your groups.
Here are some language items which relate to ambitions of different
kinds and in various ways. Look them up in your dictionaries, then
decide whether any of them can be used to talk about the experiences
of ambition which you have already discussed.

wishful thinking	pious hope
pipe-dream	castles in Spain
would-be	aspire to
strive	count one's chickens before they are hatched
incurable optimist	defeatist
know one's own limitations	realistic
unattainable	resolve
by design	goal in life
end in life	enterprising
go-ahead	opportunist
go in for	devote oneself to
urge	yen
itch	craving
weak-willed	mad for

2.1   Text A

As you read the poem, try to decide the profession of the speaker and
who he might be talking to. Is his attitude to ambition similar to that of
any member of your group?

No sketches first, no studies, that's long past:
I do what many dream of, all their lives,
–Dream? strive to do, and agonize to do,
And fail in doing. I could count twenty such
On twice your fingers, and not leave this town,   5
Who strive—you don't know how the others strive
To paint a little thing like that you smeared

Carelessly passing with your robes afloat,–
Yet do much less, so much less, Someone says,
(I know his name, no matter)–so much less!   10
Well, less is more, Lucrezia: I am judged.
There burns a truer light of God in them,
In their vexed beating stuffed and stopped-up brain,
Heart, or whate'er else, than goes on to prompt
This low-pulsed forthright craftsman's hand of mine.   15
Their works drop groundward, but themselves, I know,
Reach many a time a heaven that's shut to me,
Enter and take their place there sure enough,
Though they come back and cannot tell the world.
My works are nearer heaven, but I sit here.   20
The sudden blood of these men! at a word–
Praise them, it boils, or blame them, it boils too.
I, painting from myself and to myself,
Know what I do, am unmoved by men's blame
Or their praise either. Somebody remarks   25
Morello's outline there is wrongly traced,
His hue mistaken; what of that? or else,
Rightly traced and well ordered; what of that?
Speak as they please, what does the mountain care?
Ah, but a man's reach should exceed his grasp,   30
Or what's a heaven for? All is silver-grey
Placid and perfect with my art: the worse!

Robert Browning, *Andrea del Sarto*

Now discuss with the others in your group:
– The speaker's profession;
– His attitude to ambition and how it compares with yours.
a) What do 'many dream of, all their lives' (l.2)?
b) Who 'do much less' (l.9), and compared to whom is it less?
c) Why is 'This low-pulsed forthright craftsman's hand of mine' (l.15)
   inferior to the work of the others ('them' in line 12)?
d) What contrasts does the speaker make between his works and
   himself in line 20?
e) What does 'the mountain' (l.29) refer to? Is the 'mountain' moved
   by praise or blame?
f) Does Andrea del Sarto's 'reach' 'exceed his grasp' (l.30)?
g) Why does he say 'the worse' (l.32) about his own technical perfection in art?
h) Do you think he is resigned to being what he is, and not reaching 'a
   heaven that's shut to me' (l.17)?

2.2 Think back to the experiences you shared with your group. Do they show that you know your own limitations, as Andrea del Sarto did? Is it a good quality, or should we strive to be and do more? Has anyone ever criticised your limitations, for example in a school report? What was your reaction? Did the criticism make you more, or less, ambitious? Write a few paragraphs about your own attitudes to ambition, giving examples from your own experience.

2.3 Class discussion.
Is the aspiring spirit of the artist more important than the perfection of the work of art? The Victorian critic John Ruskin wrote 'No great man ever stops working until he has reached his point of failure; that is to say, his mind is always far in advance of his powers of execution' (*The Stones of Venice*). Is this similar to what Browning says in lines 30–31? Can there be any such thing as perfection, in your opinion?

3.1 Text B 🔲

We all have ambitions for ourselves of some kind. The next extract, however, shows one person's ambitions for another. Do you think that Sybil's mind is 'in advance' of Jim's 'powers of execution'?

Her love was trembling in laughter on her lips. She was thinking of Prince Charming, and, that she might think of him all the more, she did not talk of him but prattled on about the ship in which Jim was going to sail, about the gold he was certain to find, about the $_5$ wonderful heiress whose life he was to save from the wicked, red-shirted bushrangers. For he was not to remain a sailor, or a super-cargo, or whatever he was going to be. Oh, no! A sailor's existence was dreadful. Fancy being cooped up in a horrid ship, with the $_{10}$ hoarse, hump-backed waves trying to get in, and a black wind blowing the masts down, and tearing the sails into long screaming ribands! He was to leave the vessel at Melbourne, bid a polite good-bye to the captain, and go off at once to the gold-fields. Before a $_{15}$ week was over he was to come across a large nugget of pure gold, the largest nugget that had ever been discovered, and bring it down to the coast in a wagon guarded by six mounted policemen. The bushrangers were to attack them three times, and be defeated with immense slaughter. Or, no. He was not to go to the gold-fields at all. They were horrid places, where men got intoxicated, and shot each other in bar-rooms, and used bad language. He was to be a nice sheep-farmer, and one evening, as he was riding home, he was to see the beautiful heiress being carried off by a robber on a black horse, and give chase, and rescue her. Of course she would fall in love with him, and he with her, and they would get married, and come home, and live in an immense house in London. Yes, there were delightful things in store for him. But he must be very good, and not lose his temper, or spend his money foolishly. She was only a year older than he was, but she knew so much more of life. He must be sure, also, to write to her by every mail, and to say his prayers each night before he went to sleep. God was very good, and would watch over him. She would pray for him, too, and in a few years he would come back quite rich and happy.

Oscar Wilde, *The Picture of Dorian Gray*

a) Describe the nature of Sybil's fantasy of Jim's future. Is it realistic or totally impossible, or somewhere between?
b) How would *you* react if you were Jim listening to Sybil 'prattling on'? Would the fantasy excite you or depress you? Why?
c) There are some negative fantasies as well as positive ones. What do they have in common?
d) What do her fantastic ambitions for Jim tell us about Sybil?

3.2 Class discussion.
Sybil's fantasy seems to equate wealth with happiness. Do you think they go together?

4.1 Text C 📼

Split up into seven pairs or groups (or work individually). Read the extract from Gray's *Elegy Written in a Country Churchyard* that is assigned to you, and discuss the points that follow your extract.

Group 1

The Curfew tolls the knell of parting day,
The lowing herd wind slowly o'er the lea,
The plowman homeward plods his weary way,
And leaves the world to darkness and to me.

Now fades the glimmering landscape on the sight,   5
And all the air a solemn stillness holds,
Save where the beetle wheels his droning flight,
And drowsy tinklings lull the distant folds;

Save that from yonder ivy-mantled tow'r
The mopeing owl does to the moon complain   10
Of such, as wand'ring near her secret bow'r,
Molest her ancient solitary reign.

Beneath those rugged elms, that yew-tree's shade,
Where heaves the turf in many a mould'ring heap,
Each in his narrow cell for ever laid,   15
The rude Forefathers of the hamlet sleep.

The breezy call of incense-breathing Morn,
The swallow twitt'ring from the straw-built shed,
The cock's shrill clarion, or the echoing horn,
No more shall rouse them from their lowly bed.   20

a) Who is speaking? Where is he? What time is it?
b) 'Save' in line 7 and line 9 introduces disturbances – what are they?
c) Who does 'his' (l.15) refer to?
d) Who does 'them' (l.20) refer to?

Group 2

For them no more the blazing hearth shall burn,
Or busy housewife ply her evening care:
No children run to lisp their sire's return,
Or climb his knees the envied kiss to share.

Oft did the harvest to their sickle yield,   25
Their furrow oft the stubborn glebe has broke;
How jocund did they drive their team afield!
How bow'd the woods beneath their sturdy stroke!

Let not Ambition mock their useful toil,
Their homely joys, and destiny obscure;　　　30
Nor Grandeur hear with a disdainful smile,
The short and simple annals of the poor.

The boast of heraldry, the pomp of pow'r
And all that beauty, all that wealth e'er gave,
Awaits alike th' inevitable hour.　　　35
The paths of glory lead but to the grave.

Nor you, ye Proud, impute to These the fault,
If Mem'ry o'er their Tomb no Trophies raise,
Where thro' the long-drawn isle and fretted vault
The pealing anthem swells the note of praise.　　　40

You don't know who 'them' (l.21) are. Do the following lines help to tell you? For example, the first verse is negative with reference to the future, the second verse all in the past. Does this help to tell you if 'they' are alive or dead? Do the last two verses tell you where 'they' are? What kind of people are (or were) they?

Group 3

Can storied urn or animated bust
Back to its mansion call the fleeting breath?
Can Honour's voice provoke the silent dust,
Or Flatt'ry sooth the dull cold ear of Death?

Perhaps in this neglected spot is laid　　　45
Some heart once pregnant with celestial fire;
Hands, that the rod of empire might have sway'd,
Or wak'd to extasy the living lyre.

But Knowledge to their eyes her ample page
Rich with the spoils of time did ne'er unroll;　　　50
Chill Penury repress'd their noble rage,
And froze the genial current of the soul.

Full many a gem of purest ray serene,
The dark unfathom'd caves of ocean bear:
Full many a flower is born to blush unseen,　　　55
And waste its sweetness on the desert air.

Some village-Hampden, that with dauntless breast
The little Tyrant of his fields withstood;
Some mute inglorious Milton here may rest,
Some Cromwell guiltless of his country's blood.　　　60

a)　What does the subject of the first verse seem to be?
b)　What or where do you think 'this neglected spot' (l.45) is?　　　⟫⟶

Ambitions

c) Who does 'their' (l.49) refer to?
d) The fourth verse speaks in general terms about anonymity – how does this connect with the other verses?
e) Who do you think Hampden, Milton and Cromwell were? Why does the poet mention them?

Group 4

Th' applause of list'ning senates to command,
The threats of pain and ruin to despise,
To scatter plenty o'er a smiling land,
And read their hist'ry in a nation's eyes,

Their lot forbad: nor circumscrib'd alone   65
Their growing virtues, but their crimes confin'd;
Forbad to wade through slaughter to a throne,
And shut the gates of mercy on mankind,

The struggling pangs of conscious truth to hide,
To quench the blushes of ingenuous shame,   70
Or heap the shrine of Luxury and Pride
With incense kindled at the Muse's flame.

Far from the madding crowd's ignoble strife,
Their sober wishes never learn'd to stray;
Along the cool sequester'd vale of life   75
They kept the noiseless tenor of their way.

a) Where is the verb which governs lines 61 to 64?
b) Which verb governs lines 68 to 72?
c) Who does 'their' refer to (ll.65, 66, 74, 76)?
d) What contrasts with 'forbad' (l.65) and compensates for it?
e) What are 'circumscrib'd' and 'confin'd' (ll.65, 66)?
f) What impression do these lines give of the life and ambitions of the people they talk of?

Group 5

Yet ev'n these bones from insult to protect
Some frail memorial still erected nigh,
With uncouth rhimes and shapeless sculpture deck'd,
Implores the passing tribute of a sigh.   80

Their name, their years, spelt by th' unlettered muse,
The place of fame and elegy supply:
And many a holy text around she strews,
That teach the rustic moralist to die.

100

For who to dumb Forgetfulness a prey,   85
This pleasing anxious being e'er resigned,
Left the warm precincts of the chearful day,
Nor cast one longing ling'ring look behind?

On some fond breast the parting soul relies,
Some pious drops the closing eye requires;   90
Ev'n from the tomb the voice of Nature cries,
Ev'n in our Ashes live their wonted Fires.

a) Where is the poet?
b) What do you think he is speaking about in the second verse?
c) How many verbs are there in the third verse? What are they and
    what is their subject?
d) Who casts 'one longing ling'ring look behind' (l.88)? At what?
e) Is the fourth verse about mourning? In what way does the poet
    express the necessity of mourning?

Group 6

For thee, who mindful of th' unhonour'd Dead
Dost in these lines their artless tale relate;
If chance, by lonely contemplation led,   95
Some kindred Spirit shall inquire thy fate,

Haply some hoary-headed Swain may say,
"Oft have we seen him at the peep of dawn
Brushing with hasty steps the dews away
To meet the sun upon the upland lawn.   100

"There at the foot of yonder nodding beech
That wreathes its old fantastic roots so high,
His listless length at noontide would he stretch,
And pore upon the brook that babbles by.

"Hard by yon wood, now smiling as in scorn,   105
Mutt'ring his wayward fancies he would rove,
Now drooping, woeful wan, like one forlorn,
Or craz'd with care, or cross'd in hopeless love.

"One morn I miss'd him on the custom'd hill,
Along the heath and near his fav'rite tree;   110
Another came; nor yet beside the rill,
Nor up the lawn, nor at the wood was he;

"The next with dirges due in sad array
Slow thro' the church-way path we saw him borne.
Approach and read (for thou can'st read) the lay,   115
Grav'd on the stone beneath yon aged thorn."

⯈→

Ambitions

a) Who is 'thee' (1.93) and what are 'these lines' (1.94)?
b) Who is 'him' (1.98)?
c) In a few words, what does the Swain describe?
d) What is the Swain's attitude to him?
e) Why does he say 'for thou can'st read' (1.115)?

Group 7

THE EPITAPH

Here rests his head upon the lap of Earth
A Youth to Fortune and to Fame unknown.
For Science frown'd not on his humble birth,   120
And Melancholy mark'd him for her own.

Large was his bounty, and his soul sincere,
Heav'n did a recompence as largely send:
He gave to Mis'ry all he had, a tear,
He gained from Heav'n ('twas all he wish'd) a friend.   125

No farther seek his merits to disclose,
Or draw his frailties from their dread abode,
(There they alike in trembling hope repose,)
The bosom of his Father and his God.

Thomas Gray, *Elegy Written in a Country Churchyard*

a) Where would you expect to find such an epitaph?
b) Whose epitaph might it be?
c) Was he famous and successful?
d) What qualities did he have?

4.2 Make notes on the content of the part of the poem you have been concentrating on and report back to the whole class. Try to decide on the shape and purpose of the poem. You will need to take notes as other groups give their reports.

4.3 Now listen to the whole poem and, as a class, decide on answers to the following questions.
a) Do you find this a happy or a sad poem? Is it negative or positive in its outlook?
b) Is the poet afraid of death?
c) Is he concerned with his own fame?

5 Simulation

A large manufacturing firm has a vacancy for a young manager who is expected eventually to work his/her way up to top management. The selection procedures include individual interviews, group discussions to discover the candidates' ability to interact positively with others, a business simulation to test speed of decision-making and the ability to find creative solutions to problems, and a written psychology test designed to discover the nature of the candidates' ambitions, among other things. One task which is part of the psychology test is to put a number of quotations in order according to how well the candidate feels they reflect his/her own views and attitudes. Here are the quotations.

1 If we can all persevere, if we can in every land and office look beyond our own shores and ambitions, then surely the age will dawn in which the strong are just and the weak secure and the peace preserved.

   John Fitzgerald Kennedy, *Address to the United Nations*

2 Ambition,
   The soldier's virtue.

   Shakespeare, *Antony and Cleopatra*

3 All ambitions are lawful except those which climb upward on the miseries or credulities of mankind.

   Joseph Conrad, *Under Western Eyes*

4 We all live in a state of ambitious poverty.

   Juvenal, *Satires*

5 Public life is regarded as the crown of a career, and to young men it is the worthiest ambition. Politics is still the greatest and the most honourable adventure.

   John Buchan, *Pilgrim's Way*

6 Avarice, ambition, lust, etc., are nothing but species of madness.

   Benedict Spinoza, *Ethics*

a) You are the candidates in the examination room. Do the 'quotations' task.

b) Compare your order of quotations with a partner's. What differ- ences in views and attitudes do they show?
c) Report these differences to the class.
d) The next task in the test is to write a concise explanation of your reasons for ordering the quotations in the way you have. Write your explanation.

6 The language of determination

Those who are ambitious express themselves with great determination in appropriate circumstances. Consider the scale of attitudes that goes from resolute to irresolute, and talk with the other members of the class about situations in which you found yourself, or others, adopting and expressing these attitudes.

Resolute	*Irresolute*
determined	hesitating
firm	vacillating
persistent	indecisive
stubborn	capricious
obstinate	half-hearted
constant	wavering
adamant	
militant	

POSTSCRIPT

Ambition is the last refuge of the failure.

Oscar Wilde, *Phrases and Philosophies for the Use of the Young*

10 Meaning

What does it mean? he says – What's it meant to mean?

1.1 Theme

Many of the exercises and activities in this book are designed to help you to get at the meanings in the texts.
Have you found them all useful, enjoyable, and relevant? Here are some examples, with unit and question numbers.

- A non-literary introduction to the topic (Unit 2, 1)
- Comprehension questions (Unit 7, 2.1(a)– (g))
- Getting you to pay attention to sounds and rhythms (Unit 3, 3.1(a), Unit 7, 4.1(a))
- Sharing experiences, opinions, attitudes (Unit 5, 2.2, Unit 1, 2.1(a)–(d))
- Listening while reading (Unit 1, 3.1)
- Comparing writers' attitudes or approaches to a similar topic or problem (Unit 2, 3.4(a)–(c))
- Using the situations in the texts as the basis for a simulation (Unit 5, 6)

1.2 As you have gone through the units in this book you have found that meaning emerges in various ways – partly from what the author wanted to say, and partly from your own interpretation of what you read. In this unit you will find some characters who deliberately do *not* say what they mean – indeed, they sometimes say exactly what they *don't* mean.
Spend a few minutes making notes on situations in which you, or others, have deliberately said something different from what you meant. Then get together with two or three other students and compare notes. Do such situations show anything in common which makes or tempts you to say what you don't mean?

2.1 Text A

In *The Importance of Being Earnest*, Gwendolen and Cecily make a pretence of politeness over tea while, in fact, engaging in a 'war of nerves'. As you read and listen, try to note some lines which have some 'unexpressed' meaning in them – for example, the last line of all, which is actually a request for Gwendolen to go away!

CECILY (*Rather shy and confidingly*)
Dearest Gwendolen, there is no reason why I should make a secret of it to you. Our little county newspaper is sure to chronicle the fact next week. Mr Ernest Worthing and I are engaged to be married. 5

GWENDOLEN (*Quite politely, rising*)
My darling Cecily, I think there must be some slight error. Mr Ernest Worthing is engaged to me. The announcement will appear in the *Morning Post* on Saturday at the latest.

CECILY (*Very politely, rising*) 10
I am afraid you must be under some misconception. Ernest proposed to me exactly ten minutes ago. (*Shows diary*)

GWENDOLEN (*Examines diary through her lorgnette carefully*)
It is certainly very curious, for he asked me to be his wife yesterday afternoon at 5.30. If you would care to verify the 15
incident, pray do so. (*Produces diary of her own*) I never travel without my diary. One should always have something sensational to read in the train. I am so sorry, dear Cecily, if it is any disappointment to you, but I am afraid *I* have the prior claim. 20

CECILY
It would distress me more than I can tell you, dear Gwendolen, if it caused you any mental or physical anguish, but I feel bound to point out that since Ernest proposed to you he clearly has changed his mind. 25

GWENDOLEN (*Meditatively*)
If the poor fellow has been entrapped into any foolish promise I shall consider it my duty to rescue him at once, and with a firm hand.

CECILY (*Thoughtfully and sadly*) 30
Whatever unfortunate entanglement my dear boy may have got into, I will never reproach him with it after we are married.

GWENDOLEN
Do you allude to me, Miss Cardew, as an entanglement? You 35
are presumptuous. On an occasion of this kind it becomes more than a moral duty to speak one's mind. It becomes a pleasure.

CECILY
Do you suggest, Miss Fairfax, that I entrapped Ernest into 40
an engagement? How dare you? This is no time for wearing the shallow mask of manners. When I see a spade I call it a spade.

GWENDOLEN (*Satirically*)

I am glad to say that I have never seen a spade. It is obvious   45
that our social spheres have been widely different.

Enter MERRIMAN, *followed by the* FOOTMAN. *He carries a salver,
table cloth, and plate stand.* CECILY *is about to retort. The presence
of the servants exercises a restraining influence, under which both*   50
girls chafe

MERRIMAN

Shall I lay tea here as usual, miss?

CECILY (*Sternly, in a calm voice*)

Yes, as usual.

MERRIMAN *begins to clear table and lay cloth. A long pause.* CECILY   55
and GWENDOLEN *glare at each other*

GWENDOLEN

Are there many interesting walks in the vicinity, Miss Cardew?

CECILY

Oh! Yes! a great many. From the top of one of the hills quite   60
close one can see five counties.

GWENDOLEN

Five counties! I don't think I should like that. I hate crowds.

CECILY (*Sweetly*)

I suppose that is why you live in town?   65

GWENDOLEN *bites her lip, and beats her foot nervously with her
parasol*

GWENDOLEN (*Looking round*)

Quite a well-kept garden this is, Miss Cardew.

CECILY   70

So glad you like it, Miss Fairfax.

GWENDOLEN

I had no idea there were any flowers in the country.

CECILY

Oh, flowers are as common here, Miss Fairfax, as people are   75
in London.

GWENDOLEN

Personally I cannot understand how anybody manages to
exist in the country, if anybody who is anybody does. The
country always bores me to death.   80

CECILY

Ah! This is what the newspapers call agricultural depression,
is it not? I believe the aristocracy are suffering very much
from it just at present. It is almost an epidemic amongst
them, I have been told. May I offer you some tea, Miss   85
Fairfax?

GWENDOLEN (*With elaborate politeness*)

Thank you. (*Aside*) Detestable girl! But I require tea!

CECILY (*Sweetly*)

Sugar?   90

GWENDOLEN (*Superciliously*)

No, thank you. Sugar is not fashionable any more.

⟫⟫→

CECILY *looks angrily at her, takes up the tongs, and puts four lumps
of sugar into the cup*

CECILY (*Severely*)   95

Cake or bread and butter?

GWENDOLEN (*In a bored manner*)

Bread and butter, please. Cake is rarely seen at the best
houses nowadays.

CECILY (*Cuts a very large slice of cake, and puts it on the tray*)   100

Hand that to Miss Fairfax.

MERRIMAN *does so, and goes out with* FOOTMAN. GWENDOLEN
*drinks the tea and makes a grimace. Puts down cup at once, reaches
out her hand to the bread and butter, looks at it, and finds it is cake.*
Rises in indignation   105

GWENDOLEN

You have filled my tea with lumps of sugar, and though I
asked most distinctly for bread and butter, you have given
me cake. I am known for the gentleness of my disposition,
and the extraordinary sweetness of my nature, but I warn   110
you, Miss Cardew, you may go too far.

CECILY (*Rising*)

To save my poor, innocent, trusting boy from the machinations
of any other girl there are no lengths to which I would not go.

GWENDOLEN   115

From the moment I saw you I distrusted you. I felt that you
were false and deceitful. I am never deceived in such matters.
My first impressions of people are inevitably right.

CECILY

It seems to me, Miss Fairfax, that I am trespassing on your   120
valuable time. No doubt you have many other calls of a
similar character to make in the neighbourhood.

Oscar Wilde, *The Importance of Being Earnest*

Compare your notes on 'unexpressed' meanings.
a) Why do they address each other as 'Miss', having first used 'Dearest'
and 'Dear'?
b) Why do they both bring out their diaries? Is Gwendolen's diary
'sensational'?
c) What indications can you find of Gwendolen's town-bred 'superiority'?
d) Cecily mentions 'the shallow mask of manners' (l.42). Does the
scene that follows confirm or go against her attitude to this 'mask'?
e) 'Entrapped' (ll.27,40) and 'entanglement' (ll.31,35) are strong
words, used by one of the women against the other. Note down
other such words which the characters use to score points off each
other.
f) How do the stage directions ('sweetly', 'superciliously', etc.) affect
the overall meaning of the scene?

2.2 Compare the situation in the Wilde passage to the situations you made notes on and discussed in 1.2. If you had read the passage first, would it have thrown light on your experience, and influenced your interpretations of it?

3.1 Text B

Another form of 'hidden' meaning can be found in riddles. Since a riddle is intended to make a person use his wits, its meaning, or solution, is hidden as well as possible by the author. Jane Austen's characters in *Emma* have some fun with them: you might find the riddles here rather difficult – the first (ll.10–13) means 'woman' (a punning combination of 'woe' in the first line and 'man' in the second, making the 'whole'). See if you can work out why the second means 'courtship'.

Mr Elton was the only one whose assistance she asked. He was invited to contribute any really good enigmas, charades or conundrums, that he might recollect; and she had the pleasure of seeing him most intently at work with his recollections; and at the same time, as she could perceive, most earnestly careful that nothing   5 ungallant, nothing that did not breathe a compliment to the sex, should pass his lips. They owed to him their two or three politest puzzles; and the joy and exultation with which at last he recalled, and rather sentimentally recited, that well-known charade:

        My first doth affliction denote,   10
            Which my second is destin'd to feel,
        And my whole is the best antidote
           That affliction to soften and heal

made her quite sorry to acknowledge that they had transcribed it some pages ago already.   15

"Why will not you write one yourself for us, Mr Elton?" said she; "that is the only security for its freshness; and nothing could be easier to you."

"Oh no; he had never written, hardly ever, anything of the kind in his life. The stupidest fellow! He was afraid not even Miss   20 Woodhouse" – he stopped a moment – "or Miss Smith could inspire him."

The very next day, however, produced some proof of inspiration. He called for a few moments, just to leave a piece of paper on the table containing, as he said, a charade which a friend of his had   25 addressed to a young lady, the object of his admiration; but which, from his manner, Emma was immediately convinced must be his own.   ⟫→

"I do not offer it for Miss Smith's collection," said he. "Being my friend's, I have no right to expose it in any degree to the public eye, but perhaps you may not dislike looking at it." 30

The speech was more to Emma than to Harriet, which Emma could understand. There was deep consciousness about him, and he found it easier to meet her eye than her friend's. He was gone the next moment. After another moment's pause: 35

"Take it," said Emma, smiling, and pushing the paper towards Harriet, "it is for you. Take your own."

But Harriet was in a tremor, and could not touch it; and Emma, never loth to be first, was obliged to examine it herself.

To Miss——— 40

CHARADE

My first displays the wealth and pomp of kings,
    Lords of the earth! their luxury and ease.
Another view of man my second brings,
    Behold him there, the monarch of the seas! 45

But ah! united, what reverse we have!
    Man's boasted power and freedom, all are flown:
Lord of the earth and sea, he bends a slave,
    And woman, lovely woman, reigns alone.

Thy ready wit the word will soon supply, 50
May its approval beam in that soft eye!

Jane Austen, *Emma*

a) How do the two riddles relate to the situation in the passage?
b) How many characters are there in the passage? Who are they? Is Miss Woodhouse Emma or Harriet?
c) Which of the women do you think Mr Elton is in love with?
d) Would Emma agree with your last answer?

3.2 Throughout this book, you have been 'reading between the lines' – digging out meanings, interpreting. Looking back at the texts, which ones do you feel you have been most successful with? Which did you find most difficult? Did you ever give up? Why? Are there any aspects and uses of language which are more difficult than others to come to grips with? Are there any texts you would describe as 'obscure'? Are writers wilfully obscure at times?

4.1 Text C

Of course, it is sometimes wrong to read too much meaning into an author's work. Samuel Beckett's work attracts a lot of critics who interpret it exaggeratedly and, as William Cowper said in *The Task*, 'Charge / His mind with meanings he never had.' In *Happy Days*, Winnie spends every day buried up to her breasts in earth, with her husband Willie (not buried, but not very helpful) nearby. For her, this is quite normal, and does not *mean* anything in particular. But she remembers what happened one day when two passers-by saw her. As you read, see if you can note lines which are spoken to Winnie herself, and lines which are for the benefit of a listener (Willie).

WINNIE: . . . What *is* one to do? (*Head down.*) All day long. (*Pause.*)
Day after day. (*Pause. Head up. Smile. Calm.*) The old style! (*Smile off.
Resumes nails.*) No, done him. (*Passes on to next.*) Should have put on my
glasses. (*Pause.*) Too late now. (*Finishes left hand, inspects it.*) Bit more
human. (*Starts right hand. Following punctuated as before.*) Well anyway—   5
this man Shower—or Cooker—no matter—and the woman—hand in
hand—in the other hands bags—kind of big brown grips—standing there
gaping at me—and at last this man Shower—or Cooker—ends in 'er
anyway—stake my life on that—What's she doing? he says—What's the
idea? he says—stuck up to her diddies in the bleeding ground—coarse   10
fellow—What does it mean? he says—What's it meant to mean?—and so
on—lot more stuff like that—usual drivel—Do you hear me? he says—I do,
she says, God help me—What do you mean, he says, God help you? (*Stops
filing, raises head, gazes front.*) And you, she says, what's the idea of you,
she says, what are you meant to mean? Is it because you're still on your two   15
flat feet, with your old ditty full of tinned muck and changes of underwear,
dragging me up and down this fornicating wilderness, coarse creature, fit
mate—(*with sudden violence*)—let go of my hand and drop for God's sake,
she says, drop! (*Pause. Resumes filing.*) Why doesn't he dig her out? he
says—referring to you, my dear—What good is she to him like that?—What   20
good is he to her like that?—and so on—usual tosh—Good! she says, have a
heart for God's sake—Dig her out, he says, dig her out, no sense in her like
that—Dig her out with what? she says—I'd dig her out with my bare hands,
he says—must have been man and—wife. (*Files in silence.*) Next thing
they're away—hand in hand—and the bags—dim—then gone—last human   25
kind—to stray this way. (*Finishes right hand, inspects it, lays down file,
gazes front.*) Strange thing, time like this, drift up into the mind. (*Pause.*)
Strange? (*Pause.*) No, here all is strange. (*Pause.*) Thankful for it in any case.

Samuel Beckett, *Happy Days*

a) Winnie uses words like 'drivel' and 'tosh' to describe what Mr
   Shower or Cooker says. Before you look them up in your dictionary,
   try to decide if they are positive or negative words. What do they tell
   you about Winnie's attitude to Mr Shower or Cooker's words?

b) Why does Winnie say 'Bit more human' (ll.4-5)?

c) Can you give synonyms for
  grips (l.7)   diddies (l.10)
  gaping (l.8)   ditty, muck (l.16)
  stake (l.9)   fornicating (l.17)
  (You won't find them all, or their synonyms, in the dictionary.)

d) Why does Winnie say 'fit mate' (ll.17-18)?

e) Who is 'you, my dear' (l.20)?

f) Often Winnie omits words that you would include. For example, 'Strange thing, time like this, drift up into the mind' (l.27) might be 'That was a strange thing, at a time like this, to drift up into the mind'. Can you find other similar phrases and expand them? For example, 'No, done him' (l.3), lines 6 to 9, and others. Why do you think Winnie speaks in this staccato style?

g) What do you think 'it' is in the last line? Why is Winnie thankful for it?

4.2 Do you think Winnie's being 'stuck up to her diddies in the bleeding ground' has a meaning or symbolises something? In groups, work out possible interpretations or reasons for thinking there is no special meaning. Report on your conclusions to the class.

5 Text D

Writers use a very wide range of techniques to express, to contain, sometimes even to hide their meaning. In *Message Clear*, Edwin Morgan plays with the letters which make up one phrase, the final line of the poem, making many other words, which are sometimes not easy to make out – 'am e res ect', for example (l.15), which makes 'a mere sect'.

'Sion' is a variant form of Zion, the holy hill of ancient Jerusalem, which stands for the Jewish religion, the Christian Church, the Heavenly Jerusalem, or the Kingdom of Heaven.

'Surd' is defined in two possible ways – first as an irrational number, especially the root of an integer (a whole number, a thing complete in itself) or, secondly, as a phonetical term to describe a sound uttered with the breath and not the voice (such as f, k, p, s, t). Which meaning do you think is more appropriate here, and why?

'Thoth' and 'Ra' are mythical gods.

As you read, your task is to identify words and phrases, and make them into coherent sentences.

```
     am              i
                              if
     i am                     he
         he r         o
5        h      ur   t
         the re           and
         he      re      and
         he re
     a               n   d
10       th   e    r           e
     i am     r               ife
                     i n
                 s      ion and
     i                   d    i e
15    am    e res   ect
      am    e res   ection
                        o         f
          the                   life
                        o         f
20    m    e              n
             sur e
          the              d    i e
     i          s
              s    e t    and
25   i am the   sur       d
      a   t   res    t
                        o         life
     i am  he r                   e
     i a           ct
30   i         r  u      n
     i  m   e  e      t
     i              t          i e
     i        s    t    and
     i am th         o     th
35   i am    r           a
     i am the   su      n
     i am the   s      on
     i am the   e    rect on      e if
     i am    re        n    t
40   i am       s      a      fe
     i am      s    e   n   t
     i    he e          d
     i    t e   s    t
     i       re        a d
45   a   th re         a d
     a       s    t on         e
     a   t   re        a d
     a   th r      on          e
     i       resurrect
50                      a    life
     i am              i n    life
     i am    resurrection
     i am the resurrection and
     i am
55   i am the resurrection and the life
```

Edwin Morgan, *Message Clear*

a) The final line gives the words of Jesus Christ to mankind. Is the rest of the poem relevant to this last line?
b) If you were to write out the poem phrase by phrase, would its meaning and impact change?
c) Do you think it is justifiable to call *Message Clear* a poem? Why, or why not?
d) Why do you think it is called *Message Clear*?
e) When you have worked out all the difficulties, and re-read the poem, does it strike you differently from the first reading?
f) Does *Message Clear* have a meaning?

6 Simulation

Work in groups of four or five.
The following poems are the five best entries in a poetry competition.
You are the panel of judges. Your task is to put the poems in order of merit.

When we were young

When we were young we could not tell our dreams,
We had no words to spell our joys and fears,
Loves, lusts, desires sang loud within our blood,
None heard their music or our silent tears.

Silent we knew despair and ecstasy,
Richer and deeper without stain of words;
Language had not corrupted what we felt,
Our lives and lusts were pure because unheard.

Older, we lose our primal, wordless ease
In joy, delight, despair; language smears
Inky fingers on emotions' pages
And wordy lies distort our lives and fears.

Opening the Cage:
14 variations on 14 words

I have nothing to say and I am saying it and that is poetry. John Cage

I have to say poetry and is that nothing and am I saying it
I am and I have poetry to say and is that nothing saying it
I am nothing and I have poetry to say and that is saying it
I that am saying poetry have nothing and it is I and to say
And I say that I am to have poetry and saying it is nothing
I am poetry and nothing and saying it is to say that I have
To have nothing is poetry and I am saying that and I say it
Poetry is saying I have nothing and I am to say that and it
Saying nothing I am poetry and I have to say that and it is
It is and I am and I have poetry saying say that to nothing
It is saying poetry to nothing and I say I have and am that
Poetry is saying I have it and I am nothing and to say that
And that nothing is poetry I am saying and I have to say it
Saying poetry is nothing and to that I say I am and have it

Contact

We tried to find a synonym for love
And counted many tongues upon our hands,
But none defined the something that we felt
And none was but an obstacle to lands
Of light and darkness which were swayed
By tides obeying laws we understand
In meeting mouth to mouth and eye to eye.

And so we met, and so became the lords
Of greater tongues than man's poor house of words.

On no work of words

On no work of words now for three lean months in the bloody
Belly of the rich year and the big purse of my body
I bitterly take to task my poverty and craft:

To take to give is all, return what is hungrily given
Puffing the pounds of manna up through the dew to heaven,
The lovely gift of the gab bangs back on a blind shaft.

To lift to leave from the treasures of man is pleasing death
That will rake at last all currencies of the marked breath
And count the taken, forsaken mysteries in a bad dark.

To surrender now is to pay the expensive ogre twice.
Ancient woods of my blood, dash down to the nut of the seas
If I take to burn or return this world which is each man's work.

Arrival

Is a note in the margin called for?
Do we need an explanation?

Why the hell should I annotate?
Is this or that a quote from somewhere?

It's all questions, isn't it?
What do you expect?

And, we'll never know now
If there's anything more.

Is this it, then?
Is this what we came here for?

Cast off a weight of cultural baggage
And an attendant wait

Of questioning. Is 'it all' life?
If not, what is it all?

Or is it all too obvious
Grief and solitude abounding?

Well, we'll never know now
If there's anything more.

Is this it, then?
Is this what we came here for?

a) Discuss the ways in which the poems convey their meanings.
b) Decide which poem conveys its meaning most effectively.
c) Decide on an order of merit for the other four.
d) Announce your results to the other groups and compare results. Did you come to similar conclusions about the ways the poems convey their meanings? Are your interpretations similar?

Read the postscript by A.E. Housman. Do you agree?

POSTSCRIPT

Even when poetry has a meaning, as it usually has, it may be inadvisable to draw it out...Perfect understanding will sometimes almost extinguish pleasure.

A.E. Housman, *The Name and Nature of Poetry*

Acknowledgements

The authors and publishers are grateful to the authors, publishers and others who have given permission for the use of copyright material identified in the text. It has not been possible to identify the sources of all the material used and in such cases the publishers would welcome information from copyright owners.

'Father and Son' on p. 1, words and music by Cat Stevens, reproduced by kind permission of Freshwater Music Ltd; Arnold Wesker, Jonathan Cape Ltd and Harper & Row, Publishers, Inc. for the extract on pp. 7–8 from *Chicken Soup with Barley*, play copyright © 1959, 1960 by Arnold Wesker, recording permission by Penguin Books Ltd; Methuen London Ltd and Grove Press, Inc. for the extract on pp. 9–10 from *A Night Out* by Harold Pinter, recording permission by ACTAC (Theatrical and Cinematic) Ltd; *The Ecologist* for the extract on p. 16; the Controller of Her Majesty's Stationery Office for *Going, Going* on pp. 20–21 by Philip Larkin from *How do you want to live?*; Associated Book Publishers Ltd and Harcourt Brace Jovanovich, Inc. for the extract on pp. 23–24, excerpted and recorded from *Civilized Man's Eight Deadly Sins* by Konrad Lorenz copyright © 1973 by R. Piper & Co. Verlag, English translation copyright © 1974 by Konrad Lorenz; Hutchinson Publishing Group Ltd for the extract on p. 26 from *The Dogs of War* by Frederick Forsyth © 1974 Danesbrook Productions Ltd; the drawing from *Asterix and the Chieftain's Shield* on pp. 27–28 © 1983 Editions Albert René/Goscinny-Uderzo; *Everyone Sang* by Siegfried Sassoon on p. 31 from *Collected Poems* by permission of George Sassoon and Viking Penguin, Inc., copyright 1918, 1920, by E.P. Dutton & Co., copyright 1936, 1946, 1947, 1948 by Siegfried Sassoon; Chelsea House Publishers for the extract on p. 33 from *Winston Churchill: Collected Speeches 1897–1963* edited by Robert Rhodes James; *The New Yorker* for the drawing by Koren on p. 34; Ian McEwan, Jonathan Cape Ltd and Simon & Schuster, a division of Gulf and Western Corporation, for the extract on pp. 37–38 from *Dead As They Come* from *In Between the Sheets* © 1979 by Ian McEwan; Simon & Schuster for the extract on pp. 42–44 from *Our Bodies Ourselves* © 1971, 1973, 1976 by The Boston Women's Health Book Collective, Inc.; A.L.I. Press Agency Ltd for the cartoon on

p. 45; Celia Haddon and *Good Housekeeping* for the extract on
p. 45; *The Sunday Times* for the extract on p. 46; Gordon Stowell
and *She* for the cartoon on p. 46; Weidenfeld (Publishers) Ltd for
the photograph on p. 48; A.M. Heath & Co. Ltd, the estate of the
late Sonia Brownell Orwell, Martin Secker & Warburg Ltd, and
Harcourt Brace Jovanovich, Inc. for the extract on pp. 53–54
from *Nineteen Eighty-Four* by George Orwell, copyright 1949 by
Harcourt Brace Jovanovich, Inc., renewed 1977 by Sonia Brownell
Orwell; Joseph Heller, A.M. Heath & Co. Ltd, Jonathan Cape Ltd
and Candida Donadio & Associates, Inc. for the extract on pp.
54–55 from *Catch-22*, © 1961 by Joseph Heller; Methuen London
Ltd, Margaret Ramsey Ltd and Grove Press, Inc. for the extract
from *Loot* by Joe Orton on pp. 56–58, recording permission by
Thorn EMI Films Ltd; Dan Samuel for the posters photograph on
p. 60; Methuen London Ltd and Curtis Brown Ltd for the extract
on pp. 63–64 from *Down There On A Visit* © 1962 Christopher
Isherwood; Faber and Faber Ltd and Random House, Inc. for
Musée des Beaux Arts on pp. 65–66 from *Collected Poems* by
W.H. Auden, recording permission by Curtis Brown Ltd; David
Higham Associates Ltd for *A Refusal to Mourn the Death, by Fire,
of a Child in London* by Dylan Thomas; A.M. Heath & Co. Ltd,
the estate of the late Sonia Brownell Orwell, Martin Secker &
Warburg Ltd and Harcourt Brace Jovanovich, Inc. for the extract
on pp. 71–72 from *Animal Farm* by George Orwell, copyright
1946 by Harcourt Brace Jovanovich, Inc., renewed 1974 by Sonia
Brownell Orwell; Iris Murdoch, Chatto and Windus Ltd and
Viking Penguin Inc. for the extract on p.78 from *The Sacred and
Profane Love Machine* © 1974 by Iris Murdoch; George Allen &
Unwin (Publishers) Ltd for the extract on p. 81 from *Auto-
biography* by Bertrand Russell; Hodder & Stoughton Ltd and
Anthony Sheil Associates Ltd for the extract on p. 93 from *I Didn't
Know You Cared* by Peter Tinniswood; Faber and Faber Ltd and
Grove Press, Inc. for the extract on p. 111 from *Happy Days* by
Samuel Beckett © 1961 by Grove Press, Inc.; Edinburgh University
Press for *Message Clear* on p. 113 by Edwin Morgan, from *The
Second Life*; Carcanet Press Ltd for *Opening the Cage* on p. 115 by
Edwin Morgan, from *Poems of Thirty Years*; David Higham
Associates Ltd and New Directions Publishing Corporation for *On
no work of words* on p. 116 by Dylan Thomas, from *Poems of
Dylan Thomas* © 1953 by Dylan Thomas.

Photographs: Chris Schwarz p. 1; Topham Picture Library pp. 1
and 36; Sally and Richard Greenhill, Photographers pp. 1 and 36;
Camera Press pp. 15 (Colin Jones) and 36; Mike Shaw Associates

pp. 18–19; C.S. Middleton pp. 18–19; Mary Evans Picture Library
p. 36; ACL Bruxelles and Musées Royaux des Beaux Arts p. 65;
Rex Features p. 70; Cambridge University Library p. 80.
Cartoon on p. 105 by Peter Kneebone

Actors on the recording: Judy Bennett, Michael Burrell, Charles
Collingwood, John Graham, John Leeson, Raymond Sawyer,
Barrie Shore.

Book design by Peter Ducker MSTD